Beau Theriot
VIEWS FROM THE TERRACE

Creating without Reservation

*That is my home of love: if I have ranged,
Like him that travels I will return again.*

—William Shakespeare

Beau Theriot
VIEWS FROM THE TERRACE
Creating without Reservation

by
Micki McClelland
with
Beau Theriot

Photography by
James M. Innes
Rob Muir
Juan de Dios Trevino

Beau Theriot
VIEWS FROM THE TERRACE
Creating without Reservation

by Micki McClelland
with Beau Theriot

Published by Beau Theriot
Brownstone Gallery
Houston, Texas

© 2003 by Beau Theriot

Library of Congress Catalog Number:
    2002094319
ISBN: 0-9721551-0-4

Edited, Designed, and
Manufactured by

FRP

P.O. Box 305142
Nashville, Tennessee 37230
800-358-0560

Book Design and Art Direction: Steve Newman
Editor: Jane Hinshaw

Manufactured in the United States of America
First Printing: 2003
5,000 copies

Photographs by James M. Innes on front and back covers and on pages 2, 7, 10–11, 13, 20–21, 22, 108–109, 111, 118–119, 121, 124, 126, 171, 174–175, 178–179, 183, 184–185, 186, 204–205, 207, 210, 211, 212–213, 216, 218–219, 221, 222, 223, 224, 225, 226, 227, 228, 229, 230, 231, 232, 233, 234, 235, 236, 238–239, 241, 245, 254

Photographs by Rob Muir on pages 16–17, 19, 56–57, 59, 60, 61, 62–63, 70, 72–73, 75, 81, 83, 84–85, 87, 88, 90, 92–93, 94, 95, 96, 100–101, 128–129, 131, 133, 134, 135, 137, 138–139, 140, 141, 143, 144, 145, 148, 150–151, 153, 154, 157, 158, 162–163, 168–169, 190–191, 193, 194–195

Photographs by J. T. Trevino on pages 5, 65, 66, 102, 105, 117, 248

Photograph by J. Pamela on page 152

Additional photographs from the collections of friends and family

For the first beautiful woman in my life, Nadine...

Years ago I received a beautiful card from my mother Nadine. Printed on the front of the card were the words: "Follow your dreams!" Inside, written in my mother's hand, was a message that recalled the past and gave loving encouragement for the future. Mom wrote: "You, my son, have learned to follow your dreams more than anyone I know."

I have no doubt that I came into this world smiling. Eager and smiling. My first memory is of being in awe of the world, followed quickly by an enthusiastic interest in everything I encountered. Every day brought excitement, gave me something new to discover, to think about. As a young man, I found dreaming came easily, and life's magnificent landscape seemed filled with possibilities.

The lyrics of a song express the way I have looked at things my whole life. "There is more to see than can ever be seen, more to feel than can ever be felt, more to do than can ever be done." When the time was ripe to set out to do my share of seeing, feeling, doing, creating, enjoying, the motivation was simple. Go for the gold! Always! Having the zest to proceed undaunted is as deeply rooted in my psyche as the belief that trials and triumphs should be equally met with a smile.

In more than a half century of living, I've traveled the world searching for treasures of art and furnishings to delight my clients, designed the interiors of countless homes and offices, landscaped gardens, built restaurants and grand manors, and am now involved in the most sweeping project of my life—the development of five hundred gorgeous acres in Austin. Just as work breeds work, creativity breeds creativity; and for someone like me, the creative process fuels both desire and the ultimate destiny. A quest for the best—that's the adventure and the joy.

It has been a fortunate experience to work, to create, and to enjoy a diversity of interests and accomplishments. If asked what I first think about when the sun rises and it's time to get on with the business of my life, I'd have to say I remember the words of an old friend who said: "Make every day a holiday." Even when you're climbing to the top of another mountain, you might as well climb singing.

I would like to share with you a journey filled with, and blessed by, beauty in *Views from the Terrace*. My sincerest love and appreciation to my wonderful family, my dear companion, and to my great friends and clients. Please enjoy the story, both in picture and written word. And dream a little dream with me. No, let's go for the gold—dream a big dream with me.

Beau

Acknowledgments

With great appreciation to the colleagues, friends, and family who graciously contributed
to the production of my book, just to mention a few . . .

Love you—Beau!

Margaret Ann and George Attal

Brenda Austin

Karol and Paul Barnhart

Wayne Beaty

Donna and Philip Berber

Joan and John Bishop

Tom Bousquet

Juan Carlos Breceda

Joan Brown

Yolanda and Tony Canales

Liz Cook

Laura Cuevas

Melissa and Marc Deer

Fredell and Bobby Deutser

DeAnne Doane

Janeen and Julian Fertitta

Donna and Peter Galanos

Debbie Greenbaum

Maud Ella Hartley

John Holt

Gwen Irwin

Charles Joekel

James Johnston

Elise Braden Kamins

Patricia Kepke

Tova and Ace Kindred

Barbara and Ulysses La Grange

Joanne Laitkep

Mary Laminack

Johanna and Ben Magnus-Lawson

Dianne Maspero

Clay Mitchell

Kathy and Leslie Moor

George Pelletier

Stephanie Petrie

Linda Knight and Mark Quick

Shirley Raines

Virginia Ramsey

Melecio "Big Mike" Sanchez

Romolo De Los Santos

Wes Satterwhite

Shirley Shaw

Esther Smith

Sandy and Dan Smith

Joe Theriot

Nadine Theriot

Tom Theriot

Ann and Travis Traylor

Juan de Dios (J. T.) Trevino

Donna and Tony Vallone

Carmen Campos Yarbrough

*Think where man's glory most begins and ends . . .
and say my glory was I had such friends.*

—William Butler Yeats

Table of Contents

OVERLEAF: Beau Theriot's home, Villa del Sol, in Austin, Texas

Introduction

Please discard all preconceived notions. The volume in your hands is not a typical coffee table book. While the visions and vistas may be very grand indeed, the tour will be conducted informally. This is a personal book. One that waves the reader inside, inviting a relaxed visit with the host. Easily explainable when you know a thing or two about Beau Theriot.

A vigorous creativity energizes the Beau Experience, rendering each of his varied accomplishments an original work of art. An overview of his life reveals a crazily patterned mosaic where the artist responsible for the resulting design is one who kicks aside convention, ignores rules, scribbles outside the lines.

Soon after completion of *Views from the Terrace,* while visiting the high mountain desert region of west Texas, I enjoyed a memorable cocktail hour watching the waning sunset, seated in a garden rich with luxuriant color and scent. A haven for a whole gang of jet-propelled hummingbirds, the air buzzed with industry. Zipping around the floral banquet at supersonic speed, the hummingbirds were most ardent in their pursuit of nectar. Just like Beau, whose entrepreneurial interests take him off in twenty different directions at once—on flights of creativity, flights of fancy, flights that roar toward the next horizon, the next new dream.

In the high mountains, I reviewed the year spent in his company and realized the experience could be condensed to one lovely notion: Beauty begins with Beau. The beauty of the Beau Experience is what you will find between the covers of this book, described in words and displayed in pictures, with tributes and memories from his great friends and wonderful family. A canvas positioned and ready for inspiration to take form . . .

Beau is a visionary. Eccentric in his happy divergence from the ordinary, customary, or commonplace, he is a man who will slough aside the prosaic when poetry is offered as alternative.

Quicksilver decisions, made in favor of aesthetics over practicalities, are stock in trade. A practitioner of cerebral calisthenics, his mental agility gives testament to the idea that the brain works best when exercised. At work or play, Beau is a treasure hunter. The world is his atelier, and he wanders through it as a connoisseur of the exquisite.

Beauty remains the favored virtue, a taste for excellence defines and drives his interest, creating on his own terms quickens an extraordinary vitality—and sleep is the last thing on his mind.

When you are caught up in the Beau Experience, it can prove to be one heck of a ride. Trying to keep up with him, trying not to miss a step during the normal course of his normal routine requires physical stamina. To get in shape for a typical Beau day, I should have tried surfing. Surfing a tsunami.

I was first introduced to Beau at his home Villa del Sol, located on a hilltop out in the westernmost reaches of Austin, Texas. He had invited about a million people to come celebrate the birthday of his mother, Nadine. I had traveled from Houston with Beau's good friend, DeAnne Doane, who enticed me into attendance by pointing out that only an idiot would skip an opportunity to meet the famed designer.

I had my first view of Villa del Sol at sunset, from a car traveling along a magnificent, winding cornice that skirted the southern hem of Lake Travis. As we rounded the curve, DeAnne pointed straight ahead and said: "There's Beau's mountain." The car ascended the serpentine course up to the summit, and my curiosity gage bubbled higher. DeAnne shared a little insider information. "Years ago, in the pre-computer business boom, it was Beau's vision to invest in property beyond Austin's city limits—property still pristine, pure, and not invaded by developers. At the time, he had no idea that progress would eventually make a lateral move to the west to join him."

Sunset on the wine house

Beau's design for the residence of Janeen and Julian Fertitta

14

We entered the gates of the villa. We were welcomed by the looming facade of the structure, framed by cantera stone interspersed with wood, iron, engraved rock, stained glass, gargoyles, and relieved by flowering plants, elegant landscaping, and romantic lighting. It did not take guests long to realize they had ventured into the enchantment of an unexpected vision of a castle set aloft— set aloft over a lake that would soon swallow a raging red sunset.

Villa del Sol conjoins the best of classical tradition with innovations created by the master designer. The Tuscan influence makes a brilliant marriage with aspects from the Mediterranean. The Greeks are represented, the charm of Mexico is not forgotten, refinements of design are sanctioned with a French kiss, and even Texas gets a nod with interior flooring made of limestone quarried from home soil and wood extracted from the piney forests of East Texas. To say that the structure, inside and out, nears celestial perfection is not hyperbole. Hyperbole suggests exaggeration. Perfection need not flaunt: it simply is.

Struck by the notion that it would be impossible to absorb all of the wonderful artworks, the exquisite furniture, subtleties of structure, and gracious appointments in one visit or to see everything during the limited time of the party, I realized an important fact about the creator of Villa del Sol: Beau Theriot could teach Kubla Khan a thing or two about building pleasure domes. He was romancing my eyes, romancing the eyes of everyone there. It was about time I met the man.

We went out onto the terrace—an immense open gallery of stone and marble and ironwork and colonnade—where only the balmy air of early summer confirmed that we were still in Texas. I gazed, then sighed with contentment. Standing at the glass railing and looking out over Lake Travis, I saw a most sanguinary sun fighting like the dickens against being forced to douse itself in the waters of the lake. The cooler head finally prevailed, won the argument, and the sun was lost. A mauve twilight settled down quietly over the serene Texas hill country.

Behind me someone shouted out the greeting "Hi, Beau." I turned to see who would respond. Without having prior knowledge or knowing what he looked like, somehow I knew he would not be a short man. A short man would get lost in this place. My guess was that a gentleman of commanding presence strode the halls of Villa del Sol. I had not guessed wrong. Even teetering as I was on very high heels, it still was necessary to look up to introduce myself.

I received for my greeting the full impact of two very intense, very penetrating eyes. Here was a man, I decided, of shrewd observation, but also someone who had the capacity for great humor. Staring at him, which was very rude but necessary to the agenda of every writer, I could not find a dull moment in those eyes. It hit me like a lightning bolt—Beau Theriot has never once in his life been bored. As our year together developed, my initial thoughts were more than justified.

A Long Day's Journey Into Corpus

Since snooping is necessary for biography, I spent many months after our first encounter digging into Beau's past, his background, his files and photo albums. I interviewed friends, clients, employees, and family. I trailed around after my main character as he worked and played, watched his every move, eavesdropped on his public and private conversations. Still, I craved a closer study, a chance to have him all to myself for an extended period. It's difficult to catch Beau alone.

Beau with Yolanda Canales

He is busy, always—and always surrounded by a flock of people. Protracted tête-à-tête is not easy to come by.

To really get to know Beau, one must tag along on a trip that takes him out of town. Well, a trip out of *towns* actually, because both Houston and Austin are considered home/work bases. Beau's life story is a tale of two cities, and in those cities his days (and nights) are exclusively focused on labors creative and entrepreneurial. Lure him away from business, and it's a whole new ball game.

At the end of summer 2001, our book-related travels had taken us to his beloved Acapulco for a photography session and to Nashville for a conference with our publisher. On those trips, my hero took on perspective and shadings, new dynamics, revealing dimensions. However, it wasn't until we flew down to Corpus Christi together on a spree—just the two of us—that enlightenment blazed most keen. I doubt that Beau was aware of my eagerness to grab an opportunity to scrutinize at leisure.

Our mission was to attend a party given by his friends and clients, Tony and Yolanda Canales, in honor of Texas gubernatorial candidate Tony Sanchez. Our itinerary was to zip down from Houston to Corpus on a 2:15 P.M. flight; zip from the airport to the lovely Canales home, decorated by Beau in 1996 and just one beauty among four projects completed for the family; be ready to party by 5:00; and be ready to return to the airport by 7:30 to catch an 8:15 flight back to Houston. Seemed simple enough, if you like whirlwinds.

Because he does not like to dawdle, Beau had cautioned me to bring just one carry-on bag. Into that bag I packed three outfits, three pairs of high heels, and a smaller bag that held my face, hot rollers, and hair dryer in it. Arriving at the noon hour, I walked into the Brownstone Gallery to discover Beau just sitting down to lunch.

I decided not to mention that we had better get going or we'd miss the plane. Because of his work schedule, Beau often skips lunch, and I would not be the cause of his skipping another.

His competent and conscientious assistant, Joanne Laitkep, had noticed and quietly imparted the news that Beau had a hole in his shirt, directly under the left armpit. She was wondering whether to tell him. I took it upon myself to point out the rip in his favorite black turtleneck. "You have a big hole in your shirt, Beau," I said.

"I can ask Romolo to sew it up," said Joanne, suggesting that the gallery's ace upholsterer could spare a minute to patch up the boss. Beau waved off the idea, assuring us that we needn't worry. At the party he planned to cover the hole with his sand-hued ultrasuede jacket. Soup finished, he hurried me out to the car, loaded my bag, threw in the ultrasuede, got behind the wheel, and we were off to Houston's Hobby Airport.

Parking in the last space available on the roof, we went inside the terminal, checked for our gate number on one of those little TV sets that list departure times, and saw "Cancelled" scripted next to the Corpus flight. We were already on a pretty tight schedule, and delay meant party time at the Canales home would be severely limited.

I said, "Beau, let's just rent a Maserati and drive like hell down to Corpus." You can say things like that to Beau and he will give it serious consideration.

With no announcements forthcoming and the check-in counter unmanned, Beau went to a pay phone to alert friend James Johnston, who was waiting at the Corpus airport, that we still planned to fly, but that Southwest Airlines was reluctant to tell us when. The fact that Beau would use a pay phone offers interesting insight into his persona. Beau's persona doesn't care for modern contraptions—contraptions like computers or cell phones. Also, he remains unconvinced of the convenience of certain self-service activities, such as inserting a credit card into a pay phone to make a long-distance call to James Johnston.

Voice annoyed but steady, my hero said, "Would you come here a minute." The two of us stood at the pay phone. Together we examined the immutably stuck American Express card. We took turns tugging at it. Beau tried twisting, I tried jerking. This went on for some minutes. Eventually Beau picked up another pay phone and called his sister Dianne to ask for recommendations. Dianne said she would cancel the American Express card immediately, but suggested we keep on tugging.

I got the giggles. Beau kept his mind on business (remember, we were still in Houston). He asked me to go find someone to help extricate the card. I sought assistance from three different airport personnel, but all three informed me that credit card extraction was not their job. I returned to Beau. "Haven't you got a nail file?" he asked.

"No Beau, we're just out on a day trip," I said, "I did not pack a nail file." It seemed prudent not to tell him my bag was stuffed with enough clothes for an extended weekend in Vegas. Finding a ballpoint pen in my purse, I gave it to Beau. As grimly resolute as Davy Crockett facing a grizzly bear, Beau stabbed the American Express card through the heart and yanked the card free. We sat down to wait for Southwest to bring us a plane.

Two things are important to know at this point. Beau does not like to sit and he does not like to wait. To give his agile mind something to do, I suggested writing a list of his favorite things, favorite places, favorite memories that we would include in the book. We engaged in this exercise for two hours. It was fun. Making the list triggered some colorful stories—stories packed with adventure, humor, new friends met, new friends kept as old friends, and some reminiscences that will never see the light of print. Relating his great passion for the musical play *Evita,* Beau ended our work session by singing the opening number, a cappella. His song made waiting in the terminal less interminable.

At 4:15, airport personnel finally got around to the job they were born to do. First, the wildly overdue transport to Corpus was announced ready to fly, then boarding passes were collected from 200-plus people whom Southwest expected to cram into a 120-seat plane. By the time Beau and I boarded, the interior of the plane looked and sounded like a school bus bursting at the seams with rowdies, malcontents, and aging juvenile delinquents. The scene was a frightening cartoon—something you might see caricatured in *Mad* magazine.

The only two seats available were the very first two seats on the plane. These seats did not face the cockpit but instead faced the rest of our fellow travelers. Beau and I would be flying backwards.

Festive great room at Villa Las Colinas in Acapulco

Beau, birthday and balloons

21

Beau's Oasis on Lake Travis in Austin—Texas' biggest treehouse

Beau slid across to the window, and I took the aisle. As we buckled up, our elbows did combat. Mine punched him in the ribs, his caught me on the shoulder. We exchanged a passel of polite apologies.

Cinched in, we then became aware that our knees were touching the knees of the two people across from us. The setup was like riding a train in some old western movie. There was no way to avoid the knee-touching except to throw your legs over the back of your neck. This intimacy with strangers did not bother Beau. To the contrary, he immediately struck up a conversation with the couple across from us. They were from Longview.

I ordered a small water from the stewardess; Beau had orange juice. Southwest gives their bus passengers unlimited bags of peanuts, so we had a couple of those too. While we dined, Beau kept up a lively conversation with his new acquaintances. Above and beyond all the things he is credited with being in this world, Beau is the original hail-fellow-well-met. As we winged toward Corpus, he gave the Longview couple every reason to believe he was interested in their life story. Their initial hesitance to open up only spurred Beau on. He lobbed questions at them, stayed riveted to their answers, leaning in so that hearts, minds, knees were firmly joined. I sat back and observed, amazed at how quickly he bonds with people—for better or worse, for richer, for poorer, in sickness, in health, to communicate with Beau, all one has to be is human.

Equally significant, he does not talk about himself unless asked a direct question. Or, on the rare occasion that a quaff of champagne or cabernet loosens reticence, he will come forth with superb anecdotal material; but like all good storytellers, he enjoys self-parody and would never embark on the telling of a personal experience without having a punch line.

After bidding cordial farewell to the Longview couple, we hurried through the Corpus Christi airport terminal. The hour was 5:00 P.M., we did not know if James would still be waiting, the party was officially underway, and I still had to change clothes.

I asked Beau if he would point me toward a nice place to dress when we got to the Canales home. "How long do you need?" he asked. "Can you be ready in five minutes?" Of course I could not dress in five minutes, but I expected this. Over the months of book development, I had stayed at Beau's home in Austin many times. During those visits, we often scheduled appointments with clients and friends in the area. Before each appointment I would ask when I should be ready to go. Invariably, my hero said, "How's five minutes?"

No woman my age has a ghost of a chance to look spiffy in less than a solid sixty minutes. Just winning the struggle against tight pantyhose exceeds the designated timeline. But I always gave it the old college try. Many times I would rush sweating from my room, hair badly coifed, unzipped, tugging on a shoe, to find Beau sitting at the bottom of the grand staircase muttering that my toilette had stretched to an unconscionable quarter of an hour. I feared for my chances to appear beautifully put together at the Canales' party.

To our relief and gratitude, friend James was idling curbside at the Corpus airport. We hopped in the car, raced through downtown, exchanging news with James, catching sights of the sea and landmark buildings as they whizzed by, and finally turned into Hewitt Place, an elegant residential area where, after a few twists and turns, we were deposited at our destination.

And what a destination it was. The Canales home is a stunner. An immense greensward, ascending a gentle hill, curves up and around from west to east. Curving right along with the landscape, is a neat and rambling Texas ranch-style structure.

The world is his atelier, and he wanders through it as a connoisseur of the exquisite.

It is hugged by palm trees and bougainvillea and topped by the prerequisite Mexican red tile roof. The property gives the impression that it is several blocks long.

Even though Beau had pulled on his jacket and was prepared to enter through the front door, I was not, so we went around back where the caterers were still unloading silver platters of food. We slipped in unannounced through a door near the garage area. Beau led me to a small powder room located at the extreme end of the one-story, horseshoe-shaped house, and left me with the frightening parting words, "See you in five."

The powder room, as the name implies, had an economy of space. And, as it was a room seldom used, no air-conditioning came through the vents. I took off all my clothes to try to cool off. The powder room's customized paper towels were decorative and appropriate for a quick drying of the hands, but I desperately needed an oversized beach towel. Panic made me perspire even more. I used about a hundred paper napkins, bits of which got stuck to my skin. I was stripped naked as a jaybird, and still about the task of picking paper shreds off my arms, when Beau

knocked on the door and said, "Come out, I want you to meet Yolanda's mother."

I opened the door just a crack—forgetting that a powder room comes equipped with a large mirror—and asked if I might have a few more minutes. Judging by the horror in his eyes, I suppose Beau saw more of me then than he had ever wanted or expected to. I gently closed the door. By six o'clock, though moist beneath my garments, I left the powder room and rejoined Beau, ready to socialize.

"Come," he said, "I'll give you a tour of the house." As we strolled through another of Beau's magnificent design achievements, we were welcomed by the Canales family, met the gubernatorial candidate, and chatted with other folks from the Corpus Christi area who were Beau's friends.

In our wanderings, we overheard conversations between people, who were not acquainted with Beau, expressing their admiration for the décor. Beau kept silent—did not identify himself as the designer. I couldn't stand it, couldn't keep quiet, not for all the tea in China. "Here's the man who did it," I said, proud as a sweaty peacock to be in his company.

Beau and me

Accolades were voiced all around the crowd. Beau became pinned in by admirers, a well-deserved position for my hero. It was while in this circle, however, that he decided to take off his coat. I slipped to his side. "Remember the big hole," I said. The quizzical look told me he did not remember. "Don't throw your arms up and sing Hallelujah," I said, trying to give him a subtle hint. Not caring a whit about clothes, and being Beau at all times and in all situations, he threw his arms up and sang Hallelujah. Then we went to the buffet table.

Beau does not wear a watch. Never has. Knowing the exact time is something for worry-warts like The White Rabbit. Beau gets there when he gets there. And when he is dining on a dish as succulent as the barbecued pork tenderloin served at the party, nothing will pry him away, not even me crying, "Beau, we've got fifteen minutes to get to the airport!" While I hopped around, doing a bad imitation of Alice's agitated bunny—"We're late! We're late!"—Beau casually bid goodbye to about a hundred different people.

Suddenly, in the last possible nick of time, appeared Beau's friend Patricia, who turned out to be an ace behind the wheel. In her revved-up Suburban, we raced a reverse course back through the neighborhood, past the sea, through town, onto the freeway, ending with a wheelie into Corpus Christi International.

With bag and jacket in tow, we ran through the terminal, reaching the gate at one minute to take-off and receiving, for our timely arrival, scowls from airport personnel who were just doing their jobs. The plane was sparsely occupied, maybe fifteen people flying. It was a blessing to face forward, to have no knees but one's own to consider, to be showered with peanuts.

"Lots of fun, Beau, thanks for letting me tag along." Eyes closed, pillow beneath his dear head, my hero was fast asleep. I would like to have known if the lights below twinkled up from the quaint fishing village of Palacios. If Beau had been awake, he could have told me. It's one of his gifts: being able to spot things of charm and beauty, places of interest, wonders overlooked, even at 25,000 feet.

Micki McClelland

25

Direction of Imagination
A DESIGN FOR LIFE

DESTINY'S BLUEPRINT

Beau Theriot's childhood was not spent within walking distance of the Louvre. He did not wander the misty hills of Tuscany or contemplate the profundity of ancient cathedrals, nor was he exposed to mythic Chinese landscapes, the architecture of French castles, the interiors of English grand manors. But he dreamed such beauty was possible to see and to possess, and in the dream was desire and resolution.

It is a god, I think, who gave you these gifts.

—Homer

Disparate in type, connected only by personal choice, a resume of his interests and achievements might appear to be the combined history of several people, and not the work of just one man. The compilation, which could very well serve as profile for a modern-day Renaissance man, reads: woodcrafter, salesman, marketer-promoter, restaurateur, draftsman, interior designer, builder, landscape consultant, sketch artist, connoisseur of antiques and collectibles, venture capitalist, real estate speculator, land developer, classic car collector, vintner, art patron and collector, gallery owner, teacher, book publisher, poet, philanthropist.

Beau never settles for middling effort. When he decides to do something, he does it with ardent purpose, and does it with a creative edge, always. Otherwise, he's just not interested. Sanguine of success, this is not a man who yawns away the day. Gifted with the pairing of original thought and a fearless acumen for business, this dichotomy surprises almost everyone—family, friends, clients, business associates, and, in the beginning, lending agencies.

Even so, being endowed with a creative mind has its drawbacks. Free to roam unharnessed and undisciplined, imagination can dissipate into daydreaming, wandering unformed and specter-like through a forest of abstracts. Reined in a bit, the conceptual mind will still eschew details. If, on the other hand, vision is balanced with shrewd discretion and good judgment, symmetry occurs. Beau has this balance, and he learned early on the wisdom of delegating important details to a competent staff.

Cowboy Bobby at age two saddled up for life's wild ride

How does one become an artist-entrepreneur? Certainly it is not a field of study listed on college curriculum. How does one sustain the momentum and keep it going as an artist-entrepreneur?

Determination must be in the mix, and insight and inspiration. Of course being at the right place at the right time helps. But more importantly, a fellow must know what to do when he gets there.

Young Beau

To persevere undaunted comes very close to explaining how Beau reacts each time he's gotten there. Forming a game plan, a business plan, any kind of plan that has the potential to produce results is a learned ability.

For Beau, happy circumstance gave him parents, grandparents, and other respected mentors who took the care and time to instruct. Beau credits his wonderful family with making the greatest contribution to his success. By instruction and by example, they helped to establish the work ethic and personal ethos that forms the core of his character. Stir confidence into the mix, along with an allegiance to fair dealing, and ideals and ideas began to take shape. By the time teenage years came along, Beau was eager for a challenge. Eager to see opportunity hanging ripe for the plucking. Eager to stretch a hand up to take the prize.

But destiny has high expectations. Should the goal be out of reach, it is a clever lad who runs off to fetch a ladder. All sizes, all shapes, big ones, little ones, some wobbly, some of steely weight— in his life, Beau has gathered lots of ladders.

The Early Years

Robert Harvy Theriot was born in Jasper, Texas, on September 1, 1946. At the tender age of three, he found himself bundled off to the Texas coastal town of Port Arthur, where the family settled and where he spent the impressionable years of youth. Located at the southeastern rim of the state, nestled so close to Louisiana that the

Whippoorwill Farm family, circa 2001

fragrance of spicy Cajun cooking occasionally wafts over on the breezes, Port Arthur provided hometown roots, but the allure of the world beyond was always in the air, and always on his mind.

Growing up wedged between the port town's vibrant hub and the exotically dissimilar weeping-willowed land of jambalaya and jazz, it did not take him long to realize the desirability of peppering experience with variety. The influences on his developing senses came from genetics as well as from geography, a mix of the Piney Woods that succored his mother's family for generations and the Creole blend of Spanish and French on his father's Louisiana side.

As the third child of Nadine Horn Theriot and Ives Robert Theriot, the fortunate Bobby, as Beau was called in childhood, was positioned at the sibling center. Growing up situated between two older sisters and two younger brothers was a vantage point that bolstered personal confidence and security and gave him the opportunity to develop friendships from one end of the family to the other.

A smile was always his preferred expression, and the promise in his eyes suggested that precocity would be tempered with good humor. Eager to take that step over the edge, especially when opportunity to tease presented itself, he was voted the one in the family most likely to shake things up, most likely to go for outrageous when life got a little staid and slow. With the swarthy good looks of a gypsy, he was amiable and out-going in childhood, an excellent student, like all the Theriot siblings, disciplined, and hard-working. And at all times, in all pursuits, creative and imaginative.

Theriot family gathering

Inasmuch as a developing artist is equally influenced by both his innate ability and his surroundings—by where the artist finds himself planted—the industrial port town might seem an unlikely nurturing ground for someone who grew up to appreciate the aesthetics—a young man who grew to embrace beauty in all of its diverse forms.

Aside from frequent car trips up the road to romp with his siblings across the pastoral playground of their grandparents' farm in Magnolia Springs, his portal on the world was confined in his youth to refinery-pocked skies, flattened landscape, concrete, and commerce. Still, imagination was always at work. As a boy— and perhaps even lingering on into manhood—he saw the million twinkling lights of the refineries not as necessary illumination over hardcore business, but as the stuff of fantasy.

It's all in how one looks at things, and when Bobby looked at the night sky of his hometown, the lights seemed to wink as a million

beacons, suggesting a million possibilities, signaling
from far away, and signaling that the day would come
when he would seek their source. Although Port
Arthur might not exactly rise to Arthurian legend,
if a fellow has the interest and curiosity to look
close enough, he can find romance in every corner
of the world. Even in the history of his hometown.

Settled in the distant past by the Attacapas
Indians, the swampy, flat, treeless marshland that
eventually became Port Arthur exposed muskrat,
mink, and raccoon, all of which the Attacapas
harvested for pelts, then canoed into a booming
business by trading skins up and down the
Sabine River.

In 1900, taking the entrepreneurial baton
from the Indians, one John W. "Bet-A-Million"
Gates paid $1.4 million to own and dredge a ship
canal that he cleverly ceded to the government for one dollar. By
1914, Port Arthur was the twelfth largest port in the United States.

Allure of the world beyond

Some of the native sons and daughters of Port Arthur won fame
in the world: legendary singer Janis Joplin is remembered at a local
annual festival; Olympic gold medalist Babe Zaharias has never been
bested as the best all-around female athlete; World War II ace Major
General Harold "Tom" Collins was the first man to fly a sonic boom;
and singer Issac Patton Sweat boot-scooted the "Cotton-eyed Joe"
to national and international recognition. And when Robert Harvy
Theriot came along, he had some dreams of his own.

Looking over the accomplishments of the first fifty-plus years
of his life, it is a fair statement to say that Beau shares a commonality
with the Port Arthurian predecessors who set precedents. Like the
fur-trading Attacapas, Beau recognizes opportunity, knows how to
use the land to its best advantage, and is a natural-born salesman.
Like "Bet-A-Million" Gates, Beau is a risk-taker, an advocate of
venturous enterprise, a builder. And with the same will to excel that
propelled these talented people, Beau ascended from the flatlands
to soar to the top—to soar to the top in a variety of endeavors.

PORTRAIT OF THE ARTIST AS A YOUNG MAN

A Remembrance by Brenda Austin

Sister Brenda

. . . our ham had confidence. . . .

Looking back, there were a lot of signs that a person of extraordinary creativity was living right there with us under the same roof. Who knows what incites and inspires the artistic mind to come alive, especially one that is instinctive? Nevertheless, it was apparent, even in his boyhood, that Beau had the impulses and the inclinations of an original thinker, a creator, an artist.

I remember Mother's explanation of Beau's motivation. She said, "He was never told that he couldn't do something original—never told that original creation was beyond his reach, so he always tried."

One day, while still in elementary school, Beau presented our parents with detailed floor plans for what he called "Mother's dream home." There were elevations, scaled rooms, clarity and intricacy in the design. Daddy looked over the plans, pronounced them workable, and the accomplishment was rewarded with praise. Mother and Daddy never failed to encourage Beau, which I believe gave him the incentive to work harder. Praise, when it's been legitimately earned, spurs the imaginative mind onward and upward. It's the best thing parents can do for an impressionable child.

It can also bring out the ham in a kid. Every family has one, I'm sure, but our ham had confidence and an outgoing, humorous personality from day one. Beau got his *joie de vivre* from both sides of the family—from Daddy and from Mother's father, Harvy Horn, who

Beau has many surprising outlets for expression. I think he must express himself creatively or, like a balloon that's pumped to the breaking point, he would burst.

was a gregarious, happy-go-lucky character. As an example of the playfulness that is a solid part of Beau's personality, when we were kids should a camera be pointed in a direction that did not include him in the picture, Beau would leap across the room to get in the photo. We have lots and lots of pictures with Beau smiling and waving down in the corner of a photograph.

By the time he entered high school, he had been working with Daddy at the lumberyard for a while. One day he came home with a stereo cabinet that he had built for our parents. He had designed it without using a pattern, and had finished it himself. Mother still has that cabinet in her house in Magnolia Springs. Soon after, Beau crafted a hutch that he gave as a gift to Dianne when she married. Several years ago, I was helping Dianne move, and when we loaded the hutch for transport to her new house we made a discovery. Taped to the back of the cabinet was a poem written by Beau that we assumed he had created at the time he made the hutch. Like anything he tries that has creativity stirred into the mix, the poem was good.

After that first attempt in high school, more poetry came forth over the next thirty years—poems presented as expressions of his feelings and his humor to family and friends. Apparent to all recipients, Beau has many surprising outlets for expression. I think he must express himself creatively or, like a balloon that's pumped to the breaking point, he would burst.

The Horns Of Plenty

During the first quarter of the last century, Nadine Theriot was growing up on Whippoorwill Farm in the Texas Piney Woods in a family home constructed in a classical Texas style, a style typical of a great majority of houses built before air-conditioning. It had a wide hall running down the middle of the house from front door to back door, with rooms fanning out on either side. In the vernacular of the region, the style was called "dog trot," and, besides providing the family pet a lively and straightforward promenade, the design allowed breezes to flow into and roundabout the rooms, creating a natural cooling system—when there were breezes. Breezes in Texas are a boon of nature nobody ever really counts on.

The uncluttered simplicity of the home's design made an imprint on the young girl. Her developing sense of style found its precedent in the uncomplicated line—in beauty that is cut to bone, never fussy—and the preference did not alter when, in later years, she became an antique dealer and collector. As a collector, Nadine concentrated her interest on pieces of primitive refinement. The designation is not an oxymoron, but is descriptive of metalwork, woodwork, ceramics, glass, and stone that have been forged and hewn and molded and made—in individualistic detail—by the hand of a dedicated craftsperson.

Great-grandparents Eli and Roxy Horn

Reflecting on impressions and influences from her childhood, Nadine said, "More than anything else, my love for beams made of country woods, cabinets constructed of planed cypress, floors of natural pine, and for rooms that are large and airy came from my mother, Mary Zaidee Horn. My admiration for chairs and tables exemplary of the woodcrafter's art, for pieces that conjure a vision

The real voyage of discovery
consists not in seeking new landscapes
but in having new eyes.

—Marcel Proust

Nadine, Forest Rae, Fairy Mae, Harvy and Mary Zaidee Horn

of one man or one woman in a rustic studio working the wood by hand, came from my mother. Even with her simple background, she had wonderful taste—it was a natural part of her being."

A cook of renown among past and present family members, and among Piney Woods neighbors up and down the road, Zaidee Horn would be credited as the one who most influenced Beau's interest in and love of good food. As a young boy, it was at grandmother's table that the palate of the future successful restaurateur became keen and discriminate.

Raising hogs at Whippoorwill Farm . . . Ol' Samson weighed in at over 1000 pounds.

Whippoorwill Farm
Buttermilk Pie

*Nadine's Whippoorwill Farm Buttermilk
Pie is still a family favorite.*

1/2 cup butter, softened
1 1/2 cups sugar
3 eggs, beaten
3 tablespoons flour
1 cup buttermilk
1 teaspoon vanilla extract
1/4 teaspoon nutmeg
1 (9-inch) unbaked pie shell

Preheat the oven to 350 degrees. Cream
the butter with the sugar in a mixing bowl until
light and fluffy. Add the eggs and flour and beat
until smooth. Stir in the buttermilk, vanilla and
nutmeg. Pour into the pie shell and bake for
40 to 50 minutes or until set. Cool before slicing
and serving.

The East Texas beauty, Nadine Horn, who won Bob's heart

Nadine recalls some savory memories: "Freshly ground cornmeal to make the Christmas cornbread dressing would find the usual celery and onions and turkey drippings combined in the mix, but then Mommy would mash in a couple of baked sweet potatoes, and tradition became firmly, deliciously established. For a hundred Christmases, the dressing 'like Grandmother makes' has graced the holiday board at Whippoorwill Farm.

"Growing up on the farm in the home that my parents made together remains a storybook picture in my mind. A print by Currier & Ives. A moment from childhood painted by Norman Rockwell. The memory hears cicadas humming outside the window, watches fireflies dance after twilight, sees pies cooling on a windowsill, smells pot roast and vegetables simmering on the stove, remembers the family—mother, father, me and my sister and brother—sitting down together for supper."

Nadine's father, Harvy Horn, had inherited the two-hundred-acre farm from his father, Eli Horn, who had migrated from Georgia to the Texas Piney Woods in the late nineteenth century. At one time the property, acquired in 1875, stretched down to the Nueces River, where even today the adjoining Horn Swamp bears witness to the family's long history in this pretty neck of the woods.

Nadine enjoyed a close and loving relationship with her father, and she remembers looking forward to their daily walks through a towering forest. Renowned for its majestic trees, the area would become the state's richest source for the lumbering industry. The forest, lush with timber of venerable age and the melodies of birdsong, was carpeted with a thick cushion of pine needles, but no path led the way. Instead they would wander, talking together and occasionally singing.

*Bob Theriot, the handsome
marine in World War II*

Singing was her father's passion. For livelihood, he worked in the timber business, establishing his own sawmill at Whippoorwill Farm. He raised hogs during the Depression, and in the early 1940s he became Road Commissioner for Jasper County, a position he held for eighteen years. But on Sundays, Harvy Horn sang.

"At the little church down the road, people would gather every Sunday evening to hear Dad's quartet, and to join in the singing themselves. And four times a year, people would come to Magnolia Springs from all over east Texas to attend a singing convention. Dad organized and directed the convention, and he led the singing. The little church overflowed with enthusiastic singers, and I can still picture people standing outside, faces at the windows, singing their hearts out. In the Depression, a community sing brought joy and hope and was the best entertainment around."

The very pretty Miss Horn

Exhibiting the independent spirit and fearlessness that would eventually define the characters of her children, Nadine left the farm to attend business school in Beaumont after graduating from high school at the age of sixteen. One day, as she was walking to class, two young men coming toward her down the street tipped their hats in passing and smiled. Noticing that one of the young men was uncommonly handsome, Nadine allowed herself to return the smile. It was a pleasant moment, but forgotten by the time she reached the classroom. A week later she met the good-looking stranger again.

Through inquiry and tenacious effort, Ives Robert Theriot had managed to find a friend of Nadine's who was a mutual friend of a friend of his. When all these friends got together, Bob explained that he would like to meet the very pretty Miss Horn, and the day for introduction was arranged. "Bob told me that when he first saw me on the street, he turned to the fellow he was walking with and said, 'There's the girl I'm going to marry!' I was shocked, naturally, but formal introduction proceeded. My initial assessment was far from positive. I thought he was the wildest, most outlandish guy I'd ever met. Six months later we were married."

When Nadine named her third child Robert Harvy, it was to honor both her beloved husband and the father that she adored.

The Treasure Hunters

With five children to raise, Nadine concentrated her attention on maintaining an immaculate and comfortable home. Devoting herself to family, she epitomized the caring portrait of wife, mother, and homemaker. When she did consider pursuing a professional

And, as a bird each fond endearment tries
To tempt its new-fledg'd offspring to the skies,
He tried each art, reprov'd each dull delay,
Allur'd to brighter worlds, and led the way.

—Oliver Goldsmith

career as an antique dealer, she considered it on the back burner. "There were not enough hours in the day to run a little business on the side. With a husband and five little ones, I was ironing forty starched shirts a week!" And, according to her appreciative children, it pleased their mother to starch and iron undershorts and bed sheets too! Youngest son Joe Theriot recalls that permanent press was a godsend to their mother. Presumably, he missed out on the dubious pleasure of wearing skivvies starched stiff as a buckram.

Nevertheless, as conscientious to the nest as she was, Nadine did not forget her passion for searching out items of antiquity, of curiosity, of exquisite form and interest. It sometimes happened that a breeze blew in through the window of domesticity carrying the beckoning call of adventure, rousing a need to seek and find. At those times, Nadine could not resist the urge to go treasure hunting. She would comb the back roads and poke around in rustic shops with an eye as sharply discerning as that of Sherlock Holmes in search of the final clue. And when a fine piece was found, and found to be affordable, she purchased it, brought it home, and did the refinishing herself.

The most outlandish guy
she ever met!

Ode To Our Parents On Their 50th Wedding Anniversary

Beau with parents Nadine and Bob

My dear friends and family, please lend me your ear—
I've something to say I think you should hear.
On a cool winter night a half century ago,
Lovebirds were courting, sweet words did flow.
A good-looking, sweet-talking Louisiana man
Asked an East Texas maiden for her lily white hand.
She quickly obliged in her warm, gentle way
With a kiss and smile she said "please won't you stay?"
And poor as they were, they were rich in love—
Though simple, the wedding was blessed from above.
Sipping a Bud, and dancing all night long
To the Tennessee Waltz—for that was their song!
And so they were married, pledged to love for a lifetime,
Which occasioned the pleasure for our 50-year rhyme.

Then came the war, to South Carolina they went
To do their duty in Uncle Sam's stint.
And while they were there came a happy surprise—
First daughter appeared with her bright hazel eyes.
They named her Dianne, a love for us all,
And as you can see, she's grown blonde and tall!
Next surprise on the scene, our Brenda, a magnificent lass,
With fair skin and raven hair—beauty hard to surpass.
Now back in East Texas with two babies in tow,
They knew the family would continue to grow.
So, out popped their sunshine—a dark little tot—
Who weighed 9.6 when he first sat on the pot.
And they called him Bobby (though he prefers Beau)
For middle name, the boy's known as "Go, go, go!"

Yes, we enjoyed a wonderful life,
Moved to P.A. where Nadine became a lumberman's wife.
Then came Tommy with a hullabaloo,
With blond hair and eyes of baby blue.
Tom was a Horn by all rites and rights,
With his fine brain, he would achieve great heights!
A little time passed and we kids started to grow—
Then lo and behold, came our little brother Joe.
He was the biggest and cutest of the children all—
Look how he's grown, straight, round and tall!

Now on with our story—no soap opera or play—
It's 50 years of glory we celebrate today.
The milestone of a lifetime is joy we all share—
We express to our mom and dad how very much we care.
And we thank you so much for your warm tender touch,
For always and forever being there—we love you so much!
Now in our closing, we just want to say
To our wonderful parents "Thanks for this day!"
With appreciation that shall never perish,
You are the Golden Miracle we shall ever cherish.

—Beau Theriot
December 9, 1989

Brenda, Beau, Nadine, Bob, Dianne, Tom, and Joe
THE THERIOT CLAN

BEAU'S FIRST BUSINESS DEAL

A Remembrance by Nadine Theriot

Nadine with her pewter collection

Thinking about what we pass on to our children—how they are like us and unlike us—I would say Beau got his love of wandering, especially wandering from one antique store to another, from me. Even in my twenties, in young motherhood, I began seeking the little out-of-the-way shops, rummaging through barns in rural east Texas, and, though modest in the beginning, I began collecting.

Primitives, New England Americana, country woods of cypress and pine, wonderful minimalist pieces from the Colonial period—these were the objects of my affection. Our home was most definitely run on a budget so, with resources limited, I had to consider carefully before making a purchase.

I would say Beau got his love of wandering, especially wandering from one antique store to another, from me.

From his father Beau inherited salesmanship. Bob was a super salesman, and Beau followed right along in his dad's footsteps. And he followed along at a very early age. I remember one bright summer morning when I was working in the kitchen and in through the door walks my six-year-old carrying something in his hand. When I kept at my chore and did not give him close attention, Beau said, "Mom, I think you really need this."

There was great conviction in my little boy's voice, so I turned from the sink to see what it was he thought I really needed. With outstretched hands, he presented a pewter plate. A slightly damaged but authentic pewter plate. Amazed, I asked where he had gotten it. "From the neighbor's trash can," said Beau. Then he asked the question that I must assume he has asked a million times since: "Would you like to buy it from me?"

Trying not to laugh—because he was as serious as a Piney Woods preacher—I inquired how much he wanted for the pewter plate. "I'll take a quarter," he said.

Beau the collector at one of his many philanthropic fundraising galas

Negotiations completed, I paid the quarter, thanked him for finding an object of rare beauty and interest, and sent him back outside to play. That purchase began my pewter collection. Today, displayed on the mantel over the fireplace in my home, are fine old pewter pieces collected over half a century of antique hunting. At the center, the treasure found by my six-year-old stands with prominence.

Nadine's collecting was a hobby perhaps in the beginning, but as the collection grew and became unique to Nadine's stated preference in design of furniture and decorative items, every sign pointed to the possibility that one day she would turn the hobby to profit.

Big-game treasure hunting also caught the imagination of her young children, who would often go along for the ride when Nadine went looking for small, hand-lettered signs that promised "Antiques" were up the country road, stockpiled in barns, in attics, in farmhouse parlors. And no imagination was more stimulated than that of her third child.

Out in the wilds, up the road from Port Arthur, a cavernous space chock-full of things old and new, good and bad, was (and still is) one of Nadine's favorite places to conduct a search. The alluring sign over the door promises seekers they have arrived at Snooper's Paradise. It was here, in his late teens, that Beau made his first purchase. The gem was a Regency daybed. When the owners of Snooper's Paradise, Jon and Terry Hampton, quoted the novice buyer a fair price, the deal was made.

Money for the purchase came from his own pocket, as Beau had been working for his father at the lumberyard as well as engaging in a few other enterprising ventures. One such venture served as a signpost pointing to the future: he had decorated the home of a friend at age seventeen.

For the historical record, the purchase at Snooper's Paradise marks the dawning of Beau Theriot, collector. And still today, whenever he happens to be in their neck of the woods, Beau makes the Hampton's treasure house a required destination.

Also for the record, when in later years the Hamptons commissioned Beau to do the refurbishment and interior designing for their grand old home, the job more than compensated for the daybed, both in pride and pocketbook.

One might ask where Bob Theriot was while his family of happy wanderers conducted a search and seizure through the cobwebbed interiors of treasure troves in east Texas. Busy seeing to business at his lumberyard, Bob must be regarded as Nadine's beneficent patron. Admiring his wife's fine taste, he would proudly show off her work when guests were visiting in their home. He could not, however, be enlisted to join the merry troupe when Theriot treasure hunters embarked on their never-ending quest.

"Bob did not become a believer until after retirement," Nadine said. "When Bob retired and we decided to go back to Whippoorwill Farm to build our wonderful salt-box house, his enthusiasm for antiques finally blossomed. He caught the bug. Matter-of-fact, he grew to love it so much that every time we passed an antique shop he would say, 'Nadine, don't you want to stop?'

"It became our custom, during his retirement years, to make an annual driving trip through the eastern states to go treasure hunting. We would get in the van and just wander—through Tennessee, Kentucky, North Carolina, Virginia, Pennsylvania. No plans, no maps. We would wake up in the morning and hit the road. On the last trip we made together before his death, I remember we were in Maggie Valley in North Carolina, a favorite place to wander. At a quaint little shop on a back road, we bought a blue cupboard, a favorite treasure from a treasured memory."

Nadine's collections include rare and exquisite bottles and great American primitives.

Beau learned the nuances of acquiring and selling under Nadine's tutelage. Well-schooled during his apprenticeship, by age twenty-one Beau had tried his wings and was doing some modest dealing on his own. For a number of years Nadine had also been enjoying active participation at the commercial end of antiquing. They decided to team up. Mother and son joined hands and knowledge and took their show on the road. The road led west to Round Top, Texas.

A gathering of traders occurs annually in and around the pleasantly Arcadian environs of Round Top, a region of bucolic tranquility for eleven months out of the year. Then the purveyors roll in, parking their treasure-laden vans and trucks along the edge of the two-lane blacktop, the hawkers call to the hunters, and business is brisk up and down the road.

Nadine recalls, "In the beginning—the first years I went to Round Top as an antique dealer— my sister Fairy Mae would accompany me, and we did pretty well. When Beau said he wanted to go along to help, I was delighted. Beau is a naturally persuasive salesman with the charming manner of his father. (A friend once said of my husband that he could sell ice to an Eskimo.) Because he is garrulous with a personality that's irresistible, people are drawn to him—and when they come, he sells. In Round Top, we had a little booth on a corner, and Beau sold eight-hundred dollars in merchandise his first try out of the gate."

The Desire To Discover

By the time he was on the road heading to the antique roundup with Nadine, Beau was no longer Bobby Theriot. He had become Beau. The name fit him like a glove fashioned in the New Orleans French Quarter, but he neither expected nor instigated the name change. Instead, credit goes to some sharp-witted fraternity brothers who, by matter of necessity, neatly made the French connection, helped along by the fact that the Theriot genealogy displays a strong Gaulic branch growing on the family tree.

After spending one year at Del Mar College in Corpus Christi to cultivate his interest in restaurant and hotel management, Beau transferred to Lamar in Beaumont his sophomore year. It was there that the event of propitious name-changing occurred.

Beau had joined a fraternity, Phi Delta Theta, at Lamar, but when he moved in with his fraternal brothers, it soon became apparent to all concerned that a most serious problem loomed within

Young Beau wore many hats.

the close quarters at the fraternity house. There appeared to be an overabundance of brothers named Bobby. Scads of them were everywhere you looked. The wrong people were answering questions posed of another Bobby entirely. People were summoned to the phone that were not the right people at all. A visiting mother, not privy to the confusion, might drop off a pie for "Bobby," bringing on a to-the-death pie fight because Mother had neglected to give her last name.

And I must borrow every changing shape To find expression . . .

—T. S. Eliot

The situation escalated into chaos, and the fraternity brothers called an emergency meeting. Minutes were kept. At the end of the session, every Bobby in the room had been dubbed with a different moniker. When it came time to consider brother Theriot's surname, the group considered the patronym most elegantly French— a name deserving of romantic equilibrium with its antecedent. It was agreed that young Bobby Theriot's first name should be suitably lyrical with his last name. And so, after intense deliberation, the complement of sound and meaning was found at last. To the satisfaction of all gathered, Beau was born.

Beau's decision to transfer to Lamar State College of Technology in Beaumont was influenced by its close accessibility to Port Arthur. He would be able to live at home and make an easy drive over to Beaumont to attend classes. The drive would be made in a car that anyone familiar with a particular pet preference in his decorating style will recognize as most distinctively Beau. There is no home anywhere created under the Beau Theriot signature that does not have at least one example of the geometric beauty of an animal skin displayed somewhere in the house. A fact not universally known, however, is that his love for placing an animal skin motif in the design of things began in his youth.

Smiling as he recounted a memory that traces back to when his brother was a teenager, Tom Theriot said that the moment Beau had gathered the wherewithal to afford the purchase, he bought a car. "He was fourteen, I think. It was an old red and white convertible, pretty sharp, a '56 Dodge, and it had leopard skin seat covers.

"Beau always loved cars," Tom continued, "and there are two reasons. The first reason is that he likes to collect. He is a natural born collector like Mother. The second reason is that cars are a way to get around, to see the world, to discover. Beau's greatest desire is to see what's beyond, what's over the next hill. It's amazing to me how much driving he does. I believe that, besides being his favorite time to think and conjure up new ideas, he finds something wonderfully peaceful about being on the road."

But peaceful was not on the agenda one stormy evening when Beau was driving back home to Port Arthur after finishing classes at Lamar. Beau's sister Brenda Austin recalled the incident: "It was a terrible night, almost no visibility on the road. Beau's car hit a muddy slick, planed across the highway, and hit an oncoming vehicle. He was ejected from the car, and both of his legs were broken. The accident could have left him crippled for life, but Beau used the experience in a way most telling in regard to his character. Of course he had been eager for life since the day he was born.

Fraternity years: "Beau" was born

But after the accident," Brenda noted, "he seemed to grab life by the tail. Once he recovered, nothing could hold him down—nothing could hold him back."

And in tribute to his friends at college, when Beau talks today about the gracious assistance offered to him more than thirty years ago, his appreciation has not waned. "When I was released from the hospital, I was confined to a wheelchair," he recalls. "For several months, an unselfish team of friends made it their job to get me to class. They took turns carrying me—carrying me and my wheelchair—during the lengthy recovery period. All excellent fellows, and I will never forget their kindness. If they hadn't helped, think of what would have happened—my life would have been set back three months!"

51

BEAU BUILDS HIS FIRST DREAM HOUSE

A Remembrance by Tom Theriot

Brother Tom

. . . Beau thinks with his heart.

Dad was in the lumber business in Port Arthur when we were growing up. Born in Louisiana, our father had been raised in poverty. He was the youngest of six children and had lost his mother when still very young. Mother says that Daddy came from the cane fields of Louisiana. She also says that he was the handsomest man she ever saw in her life.

My brothers Beau and Joe look like our father. Our sister Brenda also shares that dark Gallic-Iberian beauty. Sister Dianne and I resemble the Horns, Mother's side of the family. I was so blond as a child, I had to endure a great deal of teasing regarding the color of the milkman's hair.

I remember that Daddy was a whistler. And, like the song sung by the industrious dwarves in the Disney movie, he whistled while he worked. It made a lasting impression on all of us that our father enjoyed working. He had a strong work ethic that set the standard for his children.

In his business dealings with clients at the lumberyard, our father was kind, he let people have credit, he listened and cared. Beau is very like our father in that way. More often than not, Beau thinks with his heart. Daddy was like that. Both were hard workers, outgoing, and confident—but not ruthless in business. Both were generous, perhaps not to a fault, but sometimes to their disadvantage.

Beau is like Daddy also in his ready-aim-fire approach to getting a task done. Daddy couldn't be bothered with a slow, judicious

52

Beau's greatest desire is to see what's beyond, what's over the next hill.

study of a puzzle or a problem. He simply got in there and tackled it. One Christmas when my children were young, I recall asking him to help me put together a swing set. I handed over the instruction sheet. The instruction sheet was immediately set aside, ignored, and work began. At completion, the swing set was up and functioning, but about fifteen screws were left scattered on the ground. I've watched Beau work, and his style is pretty much the same.

When we were kids together, big brother Beau was closest to my age— only three years separated us. Dianne was nine years older, Brenda seven years older, and Joe, the youngest, came along four years after me. In our adolescent years, Beau was my closest companion. We wrestled, we made Mother's bed our trampoline, we horsed around in a twenty-five-foot-high sawdust pile at our grandparents' farm—a great thing to do. We played for hours.

We had these little homemade wooden blocks, which I imagine Daddy had cut for us at his lumberyard, that we used to build houses. Even at age seven I was awestruck by what my ten-year-old brother created out of those blocks. His construction was most elaborate. It was exciting to watch him conceive and execute the design for the structures. I recall admiration for Beau's achievement being expressed by everyone in the family. I contributed by taking one of our model cars—a little replica of a Cadillac—and parking it in front of Beau's block mansion. At that moment, a precedent was set for his future.

Taking A Giant Step

After graduating from La Mar University with a degree in business, Beau began his first job out of college making the rounds as a traveling salesman for a Dallas-based furniture showroom. Earning five hundred dollars a month plus commissions, he had the official title of home furnishings representative. However, before beginning to travel through the states assigned as sales territory, he made a few purchases. A great believer in getting down to essentials, he bought a tie, a plaid sports coat, and a yellow Buick Wildcat convertible with a black leather interior.

Not one to ever consider it a drudgery to spend time traveling by car, Beau packed his love for exploring and his ability for salesmanship and roared off into the hinterlands, content to be on the road again, and content—for the moment—to toil in someone else's field. But when his success with sales garnered increased commissions, he began thinking about investing in some venture he could call his own.

The natural progression—one fostered from childhood onwards—was to use his discriminating eye to find, purchase, and

Beau enjoys the women in his family.

54

> *In creating, the only hard thing's to begin; A grass blade's no easier to make than an oak.*
>
> —James Russell Lowell

start collecting antiques. Just like his mother before him, treasure hunting became a passion, and as Beau acquired pieces of rare interest, his interest in parlaying passion into profit intensified.

Though he had been a bona fide collector before age twenty-one, his preferences became more defined. He had a taste for fine French furniture—objects shaped with classic line and ornately carved appointments. He was not at all attracted by simple or primitive artisanship, the style adored by Nadine; rustic was just not his chipped cup of tea.

An opportunity came to visit his sister Brenda, who was living, at the time, in England. Making his first trip abroad, Beau traveled with Nadine to London, alerting Brenda that a favored sight to see when sightseeing was a sign over a shop door that promised they would find Antiques for Sale. "I took him all over the countryside," his sister recalls. "We drove to Brighton by the sea, a favorite vacation spot for Londoners, and Beau bought many things there: corner cabinets, armoires, big pieces—mostly in English striped pine. Beau was ahead of his time with that wood. It took another five years for Americans to discover striped pine and fall in love with it. When they did, Beau had some gorgeous things available to sell at his gallery.

"But getting back to the shopping spree . . . He shopped London and outlying districts, and at the end of the visit, he had several containers filled and ready to be shipped home. This first-time experience—rummaging through shops outside of the United States—gave him a taste for extending the hunt into other parts of the world. Wanderlust was based on the proposition that, whenever fortune gave him the opportunity, to seek the wonderful was wonderful indeed."

Sister Dianne

Old and New Affections
The Brownstone Restaurant

HEART WORK

When Beau resigned his first position with the Dallas firm and moved to Houston, he had an idea in mind. Knowledgeable because of his restaurant and hotel management training at Del Mar College, he decided to go into the restaurant business. But not just any old restaurant. Innovation guided his thinking. Not only would he position his accumulated antiques in décor vignettes inside the restaurant setting, but everything in his collection would also be offered for purchase.

First say to yourself what you would be; and then do what you have to do.

—Epictetus

Scouting locations, Beau spotted a dilapidated abandoned warehouse in the Kirby and Westheimer district of Houston—a district that sits on the edge of River Oaks, a serene neighborhood of many mansions. Believing the warehouse perfect for the project, he took his idea to the bank. The request for a loan was turned down, by not one bank, but by five lending institutions. The sixth time was the charm. Tenacious, and adhering to his father's tenet that "it makes good sense to work on borrowed money," Beau was able to make the deal with bank number six by offering his antique collection as collateral. The warehouse became his—his on a note.

Beau went to work, and the Theriot family pitched in. The siblings came out in force to help install the wiring and sheetrock, to lay the floors and patio stonework, to plumb, to paint, and to put in the air-conditioning, often laboring ten hours a day. After three months, with toolboxes packed up and the stage set for debut, The Brownstone Restaurant opened.

If he had been asked in the early 1970s to predict the variety of entrepreneurial ventures that would evolve from his first foray into business, Beau might have admitted a few ideas were percolating. But at that period of his life all concentration was riveted on making The Brownstone Restaurant & Gallery the talk of the town.

If one must name one character trait guiding the varied successes that would illuminate the future of The Brownstone's creator, it is the wholehearted, whole-minded focus that Beau lends to each project. That focus—Beau's ability to be tenacious of purpose until the purpose has proved successful—propelled The Brownstone quickly to the forefront of the Houston restaurant scene.

The front rooms of the restaurant, presented as living areas in a home of distinction, were created to offer guests a glimpse of Beau's unique decorating style—a style that has won commissions from clients all over America and Mexico and earned him a reputation as the undisputed champion of unique and individualistic interior design.

In 1973, Beau laid the bricks and planted the trees himself, all the while envisioning the creation of a space reminiscent of the courtyard gardens in New Orleans. For thirty years, the brick-paved entrance into The Brownstone has charmed guests, inviting them to linger amidst flora of year-round color and the wonderful collection of bronze statues. As all of the pieces of art are for sale, they often disappear in the flash of a transaction between Beau and a client and are shipped off to the far and near corners of gracefully decorated homes.

Inspiration for his first restaurant had begun with the thought that dining should be an art. The thought became reality with the completion of The Brownstone, when the eyes of an admiring public glimpsed artistry within a maze of rooms created to dazzle and delight. The tranquil sublimity of a courtyard sculpture garden in bloom year-round blends artfully with a world-class antiques gallery, and deeper still into the interior are discovered a succession of luxuriously appointed dining rooms. The physical beauty of The Brownstone is complemented by first-class cuisine graciously served to the background music of classical harp and strings, with the unexpected but whimsical addition of a tropical poolside area for informal social gatherings.

Paramount to any place on the Houston dining scene, with elegance never before so exquisitely defined, the restaurant garnered immediate success. Word quickly got around extolling the unique antique gallery that just happened to have a five-star restaurant attached. Guests were greeted by Beau's welcoming smile at the door and then escorted into the realm of beauty that waited just beyond.

The front rooms, presented as living areas in a home of distinction and set as vignettes, offer guests a glimpse at Beau's unique decorating style. It's a style that eventually won commissions from clients all over America and Mexico and earned him a reputation as the undisputed champion of uniquely individualistic interior design.

The Brownstone became a favored destination whenever the mood called for a graceful dining experience. Whether seated in The Renaissance Room with its tiered ambience, enjoying a private function under a panoply of glittering chandeliers in The Crystal Room, or entertaining a small party of friends at table in The Library Room, one finds that the workaday world fades away.

Recipient of many honors over the course of its venerable thirty-year history, The Brownstone Restaurant has received the *Wine Spectator* magazine's Award of Excellence annually since 1992 for its prestigious cellar. Honored by the presentation of the AAA Four Diamond Award for six successive years (1995–2001), the recognition confirms the high standards of staff, service, food preparation, and surroundings. To celebrate the past and as a forecast of the future, the International Restaurant & Hospitality Rating Bureau honored The Brownstone with its Millennium 2000 Award.

For three decades, the Brownstone Restaurant has subscribed to the philosophy that "dining should be an art." From the beginning, the restaurant artfully blended the tranquil sublimity of a sculpture garden, a world-class antiques gallery, dining rooms of luxurious appointments, and a tropical poolside area for informal social gatherings with the presentation of first-class Continental cuisine, an award-winning wine list, and gracious service.

There are many wonderful stories associated with getting The Brownstone Restaurant and Gallery off the ground. Carmen Campos Yarbrough's association with Beau began in those very early days, and her story typifies what it is like to join the Beau Experience. It began one warm December morning in the early 1970s, when Carmen was walking down a charming tree-lined street in midtown Houston with the plan to stop somewhere for a quick breakfast,

Anything he asks for I will do, and do with pleasure. I just love working for him at the gallery, and look forward to another 25 years. We've come a long way together.

—Melecio "Big Mike" Sanchez

then resume looking for a job. Curiosity about a building under renovation prompted her to pause and make inquiry of a youthful laborer who was laying bricks in the courtyard.

When she learned that a new restaurant would open once the construction was completed, Carmen asked the bricklayer if she could speak to the owner. "I am the owner," said the young man, who was twenty-something at the time, dressed in cutoffs and a perspiration-soaked tee shirt, and seemed more the roustabout than restaurateur. Carmen, born in Bogotá, Colombia, had only recently arrived in America, and her English was limited. Not certain that she had been understood, she tried again. "Would you please ask the owner if he needs any help? I would like to help if I can," she said.

Beau put down his trowel and made the decision on the spot to offer her employment. Discovering that she knew nothing about the restaurant business, he invented a position for her. It would be a job of cordiality, suited to her gracious manner.

As he explained the duty, "If anyone in town ever does decide to come to my restaurant, I would like to serve them wine. As yet I have no liquor license, so we will begin by serving wine at no charge. Dining here must always be a pleasant experience. Your job would be easy. Just pass among the tables and fill the glasses of the ladies and gentlemen."

People did come to his restaurant. And they kept coming for thirty years, in spite of flood or hurricane—kept coming through the transitional '70s, the dismal cash-poor '80s, the competitive '90s, and into the bright new millennium. And right there beside him, for three decades, has been Carmen Yarbrough. She is easily the sweetheart of The Brownstone Restaurant—the sweetheart and the backbone. Always a tease, Beau says that Carmen's been with him so long, she qualifies as one of his favorite antiques.

Over the years, she has performed almost every duty imaginable in the restaurant business—bus girl, waitress, janitor, prep cook, sous chef, food and beverage buyer, kitchen consultant, hostess, sommelier (advancing from filling wine glasses to wine connoisseur), booking agent for musical entertainment, catering manager, banquet director—and her original recipes have become standards on the menu, signature dishes that are favorites of The Brownstone's devotees.

From the beginning, she won the regard of the young bricklayer, and their relationship blossomed. Counted among Beau's closest intimates, Carmen says a career spent in the company of her visionary friend has not been hard work—"it's been heart work."

FRENCH TORTILLAS

A Remembrance by Carmen Yarbrough

Every day, every night in the early years, Beau was always at the door of The Brownstone greeting our guests. He had created a setting of timeless elegance, and in that setting Beau set the example for charm.

Carmen Yarbrough

There are so many stories, so many wonderful stories. One of those is the story of how we created our first printed menu. When the restaurant was in the developing stage the menu changed daily, so we wrote what would be served on a blackboard. For two years we had no regular standardized menu items. It was a bit tricky and time-consuming to be faced daily with the question of what we would serve tomorrow.

One day Beau said they were shorthanded in the kitchen and needed me to please help out. I knew very little about a restaurant kitchen but thought I could perhaps wash lettuce, assist with assembling the plates, try not to get in anyone's way. While doing prep work in the kitchen, it occurred to me to ask if I might cook for him, to prepare some of the dishes I used to make for my family in Colombia. I thought this might be a nice way to show my appreciation for employment. Beau loves food that is home-cooked, so he invited me to come to his house to prepare the meal.

After that first dinner, I returned many times to cook for him. A few months passed, and in that time he tasted everything in my repertoire. And, I'm happy to say, he loved everything, especially the soups. I was honored when he proposed the idea that my recipes become permanent items offered at the restaurant. In the 1970s, we were the only place in town doing chilled cucumber

65

J. T., Nadine, Beau, and Carmen on New Year's Eve at the Brownstone Restaurant

soup, chilled avocado soup, and the fromage soups, such as a crowd-pleaser made with black olives and cream cheese. In summer we added the fruit soups—cantaloupe, honeydew, raspberry, strawberry—all proclaimed by our customers to be delicious, unusual, light, and refreshing to the palate.

Happy with the success of our signature soups, we developed signature desserts. My recipe for crème brûlée was one we had made at home since I was a child. It was added first. We presented our own versions of tiramisu and bread pudding; we did a delicious French silk pie and a Queen Mother Chocolate Cake, created to honor Beau's mother Nadine. And it was Beau's inspiration to create a variation on the traditional Mile-High Pie. He asked me to think about how to bring the inspiration to reality. I decided to use layers of vanilla, chocolate, and pistachio ice cream; cover the ice cream with meringue; bake it fast; put it in the freezer to firm up; then, when time came to serve, present the creation in a flaming rum chocolate sauce.

We decided to place Beef Wellington on the menu permanently: pastry-wrapped filet mignon, topped with duxelles and black truffle paté. It was aromatic, flavorful, and wildly successful. The innovation was to serve our Beef Wellington in individual portions. We were one of the few places in town that still made a ceremonious presentation of chateaubriand, carved at the table, served with marchand de vin or béarnaise, surrounded by pan-roasted vegetables. It was always the grand occasion dish. Crêpes were very popular with the dining public in the 1970s—crêpes filled with every savory thing imaginable, from creamed sherry chicken to chocolate mousse. One day I went to Beau and said: "We need to put French tortillas on the menu." When he had no idea what I meant, I repeated, "French tortillas—crêpes, you know."

"Carmen, don't call them that," he said and then laughed so hard I thought he might bust a rib. Secretly thereafter, whenever Beau and I discussed crêpes, they were referred to as you-know-what. After that, I made 400 crêpes every morning in my kitchen at home. It took me two hours, and every single morning, at some point during the two-hour preparation, Beau would show up at my door. "I'm here to make sure our French tortillas are perfect," he would say, following me into the kitchen. A big glass of orange juice, a strawberry crêpe or two, and he would go happily off to work: happy in the knowledge that I would arrive well before noon, bringing with me 398 French tortillas; happy that we would be trying a wonderful new recipe for shrimp and crabmeat crêpes; happy that I would bring him one or two of the new seafood crêpes to taste before the dish could possibly be served to our luncheon guests!

I Could Go On Singing

Every time Beau went away on a trip, he would come home with a head full of ideas. For some years, The Brownstone was strictly a restaurant for ladies and gentlemen who lunch. When we began opening for dinner, Beau's imagination soared. His desire was to have wonderful entertainment to complement the exquisite food, service, and setting.

Beau bought a harp. A great big gold one. Then we hired a harpist and another musician to play the harpsichord, and the duo began playing nightly in the main dining room.

In the back dining area—The Crystal Room—he placed a gorgeous antique grand piano with legs of 24-carat gold. A man intimately familiar with the traditions of formal style, Beau naturally crowned the grand piano with an equally elaborate grand candelabra. The Crystal Room is named for the fifteen exquisite chandeliers that tier down from the ceiling. The room appears to be illuminated with 10,000 diamonds. It is our most popular area for private parties and formal dinners. Very often Beau would hire a diva to perform operatic numbers as entertainment for private functions in The Crystal Room. One night the room was booked for a formal dinner party, and our diva arrived dressed in a sparkling floor-length evening gown dramatically centered with a plunging décolletage, and coifed in a magnificent ascending spiral of waves and curls. Our featured performer appeared very grand indeed. After dinner, during the champagne and dessert course, she began singing for the assemblage who, as luck would have it, were all great fans of opera, and so enthusiastic ovation met each climactic coda.

Carmen and Beau

Applause inspired the diva. Poised at the grand piano, she put her whole heart and soul into the performance. Suddenly, at a particularly dramatic moment in one song, she threw her head back to hit a high note, and—to the horror of all except our enthusiastic singer—her head met the flames of the burning candelabra and caught her hair on fire. Guests were screaming (and I must admit that some were laughing), and waiters were running for buckets of water, but still she kept on singing. One heroic fellow pulled a tablecloth off a table, rushed to the piano, and tried to stifle the flames by wrapping her head in the cloth. But the diva pushed the tablecloth away and kept on singing. Then, without missing a beat, she reached up, grabbed the flaming hair, and pitched it across the room. When Beau saw the wig come flying through the air, he batted it down to the floor and proceeded to stomp out the fire. He performed a wild war dance on the poor woman's smoldering curls.

Standing gallantly at the piano, our scalped songbird held to her notes, smiled gamely without a hint of embarrassment, and finally finished the number. That evening was one of the high-flying moments in the history of The Brownstone.

New Horizons . . .

When the nugget of an idea comes to an innovative mind, the hope is that the nugget will not prove to be fool's gold, but a strike that hits the genuine article, the solid gold mother lode.

Going into the restaurant business is iffy at best. Determined to take the "if" out of the equation, Beau's idea to set the front of The Brownstone Restaurant with vignettes of elegantly arranged furniture and artworks provided the dining public a setting they had never seen before. Enjoying a feast for the eyes prior to satiating the palate delighted customers, who lingered in the front rooms to peruse Beau's collection of fine antiques, statuary, exquisite fabrics, and unique pieces procured in the marketplaces of the world.

In answer to inquiry from patrons, the new restaurateur was happy to share the motto of his new establishment: "Everything I have is for sale."

> *Man is so made that he can only find relaxation from one kind of labor by taking up another.*
>
> —Anatole France

In the beginning, Beau designed the rooms of the restaurant to please his own aesthetic sense, never imagining that his decorating style might transcend the personal pleasure derived from room design and engage the interest of restaurant customers willing to commission his services as a professional decorator.

Beau credits Fredell and Bobby Deutser with breaking the champagne bottle over his resolve, launching the new career in interior design. Beau holds the Deutser family close to his heart in a friendship limited to the time line of forever and a day. His first decorating assignment in Houston took place in their home. He was there to bounce their lovely baby daughter Debbie on his knee and there when Debbie grew to be a lovely wife and mother and requested the Theriot talents for the design of her own homes in both Denver and Houston.

New home design, vintage Deutser/Theriot friendship

*But on the night of the first meeting between
Fredell and Bobby Deutser and Beau Theriot,
a slight whisper of tension was in the air. . .*

Fredell and Bobby Deutser

Q: *Bobby, legend has it that when you made your first visit to
the newly opened Brownstone Restaurant in 1973, you were
dragged there under extreme protest. What's the story?*

Bobby: I didn't want to go, I fought against going. I knew Fredell had
spotted an armoire she wanted us to purchase, and I did not
want to see the piece. I did not want to spend any money.
I remember repeating those lines as we drove over to The
Brownstone. Fredell just nodded sweetly—while the car and
my checkbook rolled on toward the inevitable conclusion.

Fredell: We were on a strict budget at the time, and I'd promised
Bobby that I would not buy anything.

Q: *But you'd fallen in love with the armoire. Love always proves stronger than budgets.*

Fredell: At lunch that same day two very exciting things had happened. I'd found the armoire that Bobby
and I had wanted for three years, and I met the amazing Beau Theriot for the first time.

Bobby: I remember grumbling as I followed Fredell into The Brownstone. Grumbling with the intention
to keep grumbling until I could drag her out of there. Then I saw the piece and I will admit that I
loved it immediately. Then I met Beau—loved him immediately too.

Fredell: We were all so young. Beau was just starting out as a restaurateur, and was at the beginning of his
career as an interior decorator. But even then, Beau had the same generosity of spirit that he has
today. He cares about people—he likes to have a hand in making their dreams come true. A fact
we discovered on the very first night of our long friendship.

Bobby: Very generous man. I remember, we bought the armoire and Beau was just as excited as we were
that we had purchased our first great antique. Together we loaded it on a truck, and he drove
with us to our house. The three of us spent the rest of the evening putting it together.

Fredell: And we've been together ever since.

Q: *That was 27 years ago, and your interest in acquiring wonderful pieces has not waned.*

Bobby: Because of Beau's enthusiasm and instruction, we were encouraged to learn more about antiques.
Over the years, we developed awareness and appreciation. Eventually the search for wonderful
pieces went beyond pastime; it became a passion.

Fredell: And while we were becoming passionate, Beau became a part of our family.

Bobby: I'll tell you what I think is neat. Most children do not follow in their parents' footsteps when it
comes to taste in interior decorating—or taste in anything, for that matter. But our three children
have always regarded Beau as the master of classic design.

Fredell: He knew them as babies, watched them grow up. And little did we know, all the while they were
watching him too.

Bobby: Beau has created interior design for each of them. Beau's the best, according to the Deutser offspring,
whether designing an entire house, as he has done on two different projects for our daughter
Debbie; performing as consultant, as he did for our eldest son Brad; or proceeding slowly and
placing the single exquisite piece in a home, as the budget of our youngest son Steven requires.

Fredell: Pretty wonderful to have the best decorator in the world as a member of the family.

The refinements that Beau worked into our new house made the difference. I could have built a great house, but Beau's vision turned it into a showplace. Beau's vision also added dollars to it—but, in the credo of the master, money is the handmaiden to beauty.

—Bobby Deutser

Q: *The antique hunter is just as determined to bag his quarry as any big game hunter out to nail a prize trophy. Is that how it is when the two of you go in search of the perfect piece? And, can you recall a specific treasure hunt with Beau?*

Bobby: Fredell and I have gone on adventures in some of the world's most interesting antique venues. Beau is the one who taught us the thrill of the quest. But a story close to home: Twenty years ago we were looking for a coffee table base. Beau wanted us to have the cap of a column—the sort of elaborate column you might see holding up the roof of a stately mansion or southern plantation house.

Fredell: The three of us went to Bruce Adkins Antiques—located in an old three-story house just south of downtown Houston. Walking around outside the building, where massive pieces are on display, Beau spotted the rim of a cast-iron column . . .

Bobby: The column had been shoved under the building; only a small section of it was visible. Beau asked a salesman to pull the column out so we could look at it. Discarded and forgotten, the thing was covered with rust and tightly wedged under the house. As the fellow tugged and tried to dislodge it, he told us it weighed a zillion tons. Some minutes later, drenched in sweat, he achieved success. Beau said: "What do you want for it?" Fellow answered: "One-hundred dollars." Strolling away, Beau said: "We'll think about it."

Fredell: That's when the poor man grabbed Bobby's arm and, almost pleading, said: "Mister, if I don't have to shove that thing back under the house, you can have it for seventy-five dollars."

Bobby: And that's how we acquired our coffee table base.

Fredell: A gorgeous, interesting piece—gorgeous and interesting after Beau restored it, of course—that has graced our living room for two decades.

Q: *Beau has been described as a modern Renaissance Man. His career has been as colorful and variegated as the mosaic panes in a kaleidoscope. Can you give us an insight into his philosophy?*

Fredell: Beau was crazy about my little mother, Crusea Pinkenson. Born in Russia, she had a romantic accent, looked like a silent film star, and approached each day with a *joie de vivre* that made being in her company glorious. Mother always said: "Make every day a holiday." Well, the phrase delighted Beau so much, he adopted it as his own motto for living.

Bobby: Each time he built a new restaurant, or opened a new gallery—even in the homes he designed for clients—he had the phrase written on a wall somewhere in the structure. "Make every day a holiday"—a charming good luck charm.

Fredell: He's an optimist. Beau believes if something doesn't work out today, it will be successful tomorrow. He's fearless. At certain times over the years, I have recommended caution. Whether it's a new business deal, an entrepreneurial idea, or some elaborate whim that's caught his imagination, I have been known to suggest he proceed slowly. With a smile, he always turns to me and says: "Freddy, I have to keep moving on. After all, remember what your mother said— today's the day not only to live, but to celebrate!"

With his first venture successfully launched, there were many more rooms in Beau's imagination to open up and give an airing. Wielding the creative edge and forwarding the creative urge would be the eventual design for his life. And The Brownstone was the beginning. . . .

Beau inspired and encouraged Fredell and Bobby Deutser's love of collecting.

MY BROTHER THE PLAYER

A Remembrance by Dianne Maspero

Sister Dianne with daughter Elise

. . . I see us as two bookends!

We have worked together for more than twenty-two years, withstanding the slings and arrows of outrageous fortune, and sharing the times of incredibly good fortune which take the lead in the story of Beau's life.

When I think of our business relationship, I see us as two bookends. The knowledge we have accumulated in our shared experience is arranged in volumes, and stands there lined up between us. Supporting the collection at one end is Beau the risk-taker and, at the other end, his conservative security-conscious sister.

When I came to help him with the restaurant and the gallery in 1979, I was ready for a change in my life, eager to assist my little brother in the development of some very interesting projects. With six years

The landscape of possibilities inside his head
was then, as it is now, without boundaries.
I decided he needed a border guard, and
I was the girl for the job.

difference in our ages, Beau was, to my mind, still wet behind the ears at thirty-three, and I was a seasoned veteran in the ways of business, besides being the firstborn in the family, which assumes a certain accountability. It didn't take me long to learn that Beau liked to take chances. The landscape of possibilities inside his head was then, as it is now, without boundaries. I decided he needed a border guard, and I was the girl for the job.

There have been times when we clashed in duels worthy of the contenders in a boxing match. But being one of the few who will say right aloud what I think, especially when I think he's headed for trouble, brings a needed check and balance to the table. Beau's got the vision of an eagle; he sees the broad spectrum. What he doesn't see sometimes are the complexities that could possibly foul the deal, sabotage the dream. It's my responsibility to point out the stumbling blocks.

We are very close—heart to heart. We're even closer when we butt heads. Still, he likes the fact of me, the fact that I'm there. As Beau's executive assistant, my job is to oversee our twelve companies—a job description that includes marketing, troubleshooting, and functioning in an advisory capacity. Yet, even though twelve is a nice round number, I don't think my brother is through developing more dreams into reality.

Over the years, we've had our successes, we've had our failures, and through it all, I've ridden the roller coaster right along beside him, with Beau all the while yelling "Yippee!" and me hanging on for dear life.

What a character he is. I've seen him stern, seen him playful. When he's out of sorts, it only lasts a moment. When he's playful, which is more often than not, the moments stretch into high hilarity. Those playful moments usually develop into a good story that's worth repeating . . .

Out of popcorn, but in the Big Apple with some of the loves of his life

We used to go to New York frequently on buying trips. Beau always invited a gang to come along, at least six people, sometimes eight or ten family members and friends. When People's Express was still around, we could fly for peanuts, so eight of us were booked on this one particular flight. Since food would not be served on the economy airline, we had picked up deli sandwiches and popped lots of bags of popcorn to take on the plane. We were flying very late at night—People's Express did not have good departure times—and most on board were sleeping.

About forty minutes out of New York, the man sitting in front of Beau began snoring so loudly that the sound rattled the windows. I was sitting some rows back, but still had a view of my brother's antics. As is the way with snorers, the activity is performed with a certain rhythm, breathing in through the nose with a sound reminiscent of pigs at a trough and exhaling sputtering. So each time the man snored, his mouth would open, and Beau pitched a piece of popcorn at him.

It was kind of like a carnival game, like pitching beanbags at a clown's face. Beau took innumerable shots, missed the man's open mouth lots of times, but on the fifteenth try, it was a bull's-eye. Popcorned at last, the gentleman woke very suddenly. Thanks to my prankish brother, the plane was snore-free as we made our descent into the Big Apple.

One day I went to Beau and said:
"We need to put French tortillas on the menu."
When he had no idea what I meant, I repeated,
"French tortillas—crêpes, you know."

—Carmen Yarbrough

French Tortillas (Gorgonzola Crêpes with Lemon Beurre Blanc)

Makes 8 crêpes, 4 servings

Crêpes
1/2 cup flour
3/4 cup milk
1 egg
1 tablespoon melted butter
salt and pepper to taste

Gorgonzola Filling
2 ounces mushrooms, sliced
1 ounce scallions, sliced
1 ounce leeks, sliced
1/2 cup crumbled Gorgonzola cheese
1 tablespoon melted butter

Lemon Beurre Blanc Sauce
3 tablespoons white wine
1 shallot, chopped
1 1/2 tablespoons heavy cream
6 tablespoons cold butter,
    cut into pieces
juice of 1/2 lemon
salt and pepper to taste

For the crêpes, combine the flour, milk, egg, butter, salt and pepper in a blender and process until smooth, adding more milk if necessary for the desired consistency. Transfer the mixture to a plastic bowl.

Spray a 6-inch nonstick skillet with nonstick cooking spray. Heat the skillet over low heat. Pour 1/8 of the batter at a time into the skillet, tilting the skillet to spread evenly. Cook until the side and bottom begin to brown. Turn the crêpe over and cook for 30 seconds longer. Remove with a spatula and stack the crêpes on a plate.

For the filling, sauté the mushrooms, scallions, leeks and Gorgonzola cheese in the butter in a nonstick skillet for 1 minute.

For the beurre blanc sauce, combine the white wine with the shallot in a saucepan and cook until reduced. Add the heavy cream and bring to a boil. Add the butter in pieces, continuing to cook and stirring constantly until the butter is incorporated. Stir in the lemon juice, salt and pepper. Keep warm until time to serve.

To serve, spoon 1/8 of the filling into the center of each crêpe. Fold the crêpes in half and then in half again. Arrange in a glass baking dish and bake at 350 degrees for 1 to 2 minutes or until heated through. Remove the crêpes to serving plates. Ladle the beurre blanc sauce over the crêpes and garnish with a sauté of diced cucumber, red onion and tomato.

Avocado Velvet Soup

Serves 6

2^1/$_2$ ripe avocados
lime juice and black pepper to taste
2 dashes of Tabasco sauce
2^1/$_2$ cups chicken stock
^{1}/$_3$ quart half-and-half

Combine the avocados, lime juice, pepper, Tabasco sauce and chicken stock in a blender and blend until smooth. Add the half-and-half and process until smooth. Serve chilled with a dollop of sour cream topped with caviar.

Individual Beef Wellington with Périgourdine Sauce

Serves 6

2 pounds beef tenderloin
^{1}/$_4$ cup (^{1}/$_2$ stick) butter
2 tablespoons finely chopped chives
2 cups finely chopped fresh mushrooms
salt and pepper to taste
2^1/$_4$ cups brandy
2 ounces fresh bread crumbs
4 ounces commercial pâté de foie gras
2 sheets frozen puff pastry, thawed
1 egg
3 to 4 tablespoons milk

Slice the tenderloin into 6 portions. Brown on both sides in a small amount of the butter in a sauté pan. Remove to a plate to cool.

Add the remaining butter, chives and mushrooms to the sauté pan and sauté until tender. Season with salt and pepper. Stir in the brandy and simmer for several minutes. Add the bread crumbs and cook until the liquid is absorbed. Let stand until cool.

Spread equal portions of the pâté over each tenderloin. Spread the mushroom mixture over the pâté. Roll the puff pastry dough ^{1}/$_8$ inch thick on a lightly floured surface. Cut 1 sheet into six 5^1/$_2$×5^1/$_2$-inch squares. Cut the other sheet into six 6×6-inch squares.

Combine the egg, milk, salt and pepper in a small bowl and mix well. Use the egg wash to seal each individual beef Wellington.

Place 1 tenderloin in the center of each 5^1/$_2$-inch square and cover each with a 6-inch square. Trim the dough to oval shapes and brush with the egg wash. Bake at 375 degrees for 30 minutes.

Southwestern Seafood Salad

Serves 5

Fruit Salsa

1 mango, coarsely chopped
1 papaya, coarsely chopped
1 red onion, chopped
1 avocado, chopped
1 sprig of fresh thyme
5 to 7 leaves cilantro
2 tablespoons fresh lemon juice
2 tablespoons fresh orange juice
salt and pepper to taste

Salad

8 ounces jumbo lump crab meat,
   picked
8 ounces bay shrimp, cooked and
   chilled
1/4 head fennel, finely chopped
1 green onion, thinly sliced
2 cucumbers, seeded and chopped
1 1/2 tablespoons mayonnaise
salt and pepper to taste
mixed greens
balsamic vinegar
radicchio cups
pecans
grapes

Chef Duke Lo Cicero

For the salsa, combine the mango, papaya, onion, avocado, thyme and cilantro in a bowl. Add the lemon juice, orange juice, salt and pepper and toss gently to mix well. Chill in the refrigerator.

For the salad, combine the crab meat, shrimp, fennel, green onion and cucumbers in a bowl. Add the mayonnaise, salt and pepper and mix well. Chill, covered, in the refrigerator.

Toss the mixed greens lightly with the vinegar in a bowl. Spoon onto 5 serving plates and top with a radicchio cup; radicchio pulls apart very much like cabbage to form a cup naturally.

Add the chilled salsa to the chilled seafood and toss to coat well.. Spoon into the radicchio cups. Garnish with pecans, grapes and additional shrimp.

Beau's Salad

Serves 6

Blue Cheese Dressing:
2/3 cup mayonnaise
2/3 cup buttermilk
1/3 cup crumbled bleu cheese
1 tablespoon chopped parsley
1 tablespoon chopped basil
1 tablespoon chopped garlic
1 1/3 tablespoons rice vinaigrette
salt and pepper to taste

Salad
2/3 head romaine lettuce, torn into bite-size pieces
1/3 pound spinach, torn
1/3 pound field greens, torn
1/3 large red onion, julienned
1 1/2 avocados, sliced
2 1/2 hard-cooked eggs, sliced
3 tablespoons pine nuts, toasted

For the dressing, combine the mayonnaise, buttermilk and blue cheese in a bowl and mix well. Stir in the parsley, basil, garlic, rice vinaigrette, salt and pepper.

For the salad, combine the lettuce, spinach and field greens in a salad. Add most of the dressing and toss to coat well. Spoon the greens onto serving plates and top with the red onion, avocados, eggs and pine nuts. Drizzle with the remaining salad dressing.

The Brownstone Queen Mother Chocolate Cake

Serves 10

This cake has been a tradition since the early 1970s. It was created to honor Nadine Theriot.

1 1/2 cups (3 sticks) butter, chopped
2/3 pound semisweet chocolate, chopped
1/3 cup brandy
1/2 tablespoon grated orange zest
1/2 tablespoon salt
5 eggs
2/3 cup sugar
1/4 cup flour

Melt the butter in a large saucepan over medium heat. Add the chocolate and cook until the chocolate melts, stirring constantly. Remove from the heat. Stir in the brandy, orange zest and salt.

Beat the eggs in a large bowl. Add the sugar and beat until smooth. Stir in the flour gradually. Add the chocolate mixture and beat for two minutes to fully combine.

Spoon into a 12×20-inch cake pan. Bake at 300 degrees for 45 minutes.

The Brownstone Favorite Famous Bread Pudding With Apple Whiskey Sauce

Serves 5

Pudding
2 egg yolks
1/3 cup sugar
1 pint cream
1/2 vanilla bean
1/2 tablespoon vanilla extract
1 cinnamon stick, broken
2 croissants, cut into 1/2-inch pieces
1/4 cup blueberries
1/4 cup chopped dried apricots, chopped
1/4 cup currants

Apple Whiskey Sauce
1 Granny Smith apple, peeled,
    cored and cut into thin wedges
1/4 cup currants
2 tablespoons butter
1/4 cup whiskey
1/2 tablespoon ground cinnamon

For the pudding, whisk the egg yolks, sugar and cream in a double boiler. Place over hot water and cook until creamy, stirring constantly. Remove from the heat and set aside.

Combine the cream, vanilla bean, vanilla and cinnamon pieces in a saucepan. Bring to a boil and cook until slightly reduced, stirring constantly to prevent scorching. Whisk a small amount of the cream mixture into the egg mixture; whisk the egg mixture into the cream. Whisk until foamy.

Combine the croissants, blueberries, apricots and currants in a baking pan. Add the custard and mix well. Let stand for 10 minutes, pushing the bread down occasionally to soak well.

Place in a 350-degree oven and place a pan half filled with hot water on the rack below. Bake, covered with foil, for 1 1/2 hours.

For the sauce, sauté the apple and currants in the butter in a sauté pan until tender. Add the whiskey and cinnamon and cook until heated through. Serve hot with the bread pudding.

Beaux-Arts

THE BROWNSTONE GALLERY

SPACE TRAVEL

It's hard to imagine the thousands of empty rooms that Beau has contemplated over a three-decade career in interior design. Contemplated while considering color and fabric, furniture and positioning, drapery and accessories, grand pieces and incidentals, wood and stone, sconces and chandeliers, sound and sense, mood and style, entrances and exits, railings, wiring, wit, windows, and where to hide the television set.

Always eager to go where no decorator has gone before, curious to see the perimeters of a new design frontier, ever ready to be launched into the decorating unknown, Beau has made more explorations through uncharted space than Captain Marvel. Many wonders have been wrought along the course of his space travels: mansions in Houston's venerable River Oaks, chalets in the Colorado ski country, villas in Acapulco, a palace in Mexico City, a Norman-French castle in Dallas, lake homes in Austin, a yacht in Florida, a residence listed on the historic registry in Memphis, a retreat by a babbling brook in Ruidoso, a 10,000-square-foot palazzo in the art district of Santa Fe, and ranches all over Texas.

To create a personal world for each of his clients, Beau must gather and arrange elements so that the end result perfectly reflects the client's taste, personality, wildest dreams, and practical needs. Creation demands the intimate knowledge of those who will occupy the space as well as the resources to turn a home's void into a radiantly distinguishable star cluster.

Most decorators call on a wide range of sources to find and acquire merchandise. A decorator's little black book contains an all-inclusive list of purveyors that traffic in both the functional and the fabulous. Few decorators, however, maintain under their own roof a private inventory that could fill a soccer stadium.

After making a study of the different periods that produced the best in furnishing and fine art, Beau began to shop the markets of the world, making many purchases along the way. Things began to stack up, and Beau realized his collected treasures needed a permanent home.

Beau's residence above the Brownstone Restaurant

The Brownstone Gallery . . . ever fascinating, ever changing

In the early1970s, when the collection had outgrown the limited space allotted at the Brownstone Restaurant, Beau leased a 25,000-square-foot building adjacent to the restaurant. He laid the floor with fine imported rugs, arranged his treasures upon the rugs, and opened the Brownstone Gallery.

As a premier repository for plums and prizes collected from around the world, the gallery is rivaled by few internationally. Beau's treasure house was a lulu when it first opened, and it remains a knockout today.

Quality, class, virtue, and merit define the exhibition. And for those of us who like a little whimsy served atop our gilt-edged armoire, remembering the personality of the gallery owner ensures that there will always be found a trinket or a trifle here and there to bring on a smile.

Once the gallery opened, Beau found himself officially anointed as a full-fledged, professional interior designer. Not a product of classroom fundamentals, of fixed notions, or of formalized training in the profession, Beau proceeded by the beautifully upholstered seat of his pants. He did it because he could do it. He was a natural.

A few early clients, who had purchased pieces when his collection was first on display in the Brownstone Restaurant and had requested (and received) advice on decorating, recommended Beau to other potential clients and so on and so on. People in need of reconstructive design surgery began beating a path to the gallery's wood-carved double doors.

They came to wander down aisles packed with the world's *ne plus ultra*—pieces gathered from Hong Kong, Paris, Great Britain, Malaysia, Brazil, Mexico, Italy, India, Egypt, Spain—now securely cached within his own domain. And they also came to keep scheduled appointments with Beau.

With his taste visible in every corner of the gallery, the absence of a decorator's diploma on the wall did not hinder progress in the new venture. In the beginning, word of mouth was, and still is, the only advertising campaign. News flashed around the private sector that there was an antique dealer in town who performed

Everything I have is for sale.

—Beau

not only as a talented interior designer but was capable of taking a project from soup to nuts (or from sheetrock to hand-painted frescoes). No outside contractor was needed—an unprecedented discovery.

People pursued opportunities to confer with the man with the finely honed sense of style who could "see" the project after talking a few minutes with a client—who could see beyond the melody line to what poet Wallace Stevens described as "the complicate, the amassing harmony." Praise for Beau's natural ability buzzed from interested ear to interested ear. His champions promised they had discovered a decorator who would arrange things the way they should be arranged within a designated space.

In quick order, a notion came to Beau—an idea consistent not only with his basic personality but with every venture previously undertaken. To create a whole cloth of services, he would employ a team of workers proficient in varied disciplines. "I like to think of the excellent employees working at the gallery as Beau's army. Marines of the moving-day installation. These are some tough, talented, well-trained people," said client and friend Karol Barnhart.

*B*eau makes me think of Gershwin. You know, Gershwin takes a little bit of classical music, a little bit of popular, little bit of jazz, then mixes it all together—that's how Beau designs. He is self-taught, and creativity is second nature to him. In his extraordinary expression there is no place for rules or constraints. And the amazing thing is, he doesn't miss, he never misses! Wild and daring, that's his style. To work with him is fascinating. When he's in the gallery, he's like the sun in the galaxy. As soon as he's gone, everything becomes quiet and cold. You remove Tony from Tony's restaurant, what do you have? A restaurant. You remove Beau from the Brownstone Gallery, what do you have? A furniture shop.

—Josette Mieuzet

*T*wice a year for thirty years Beau has made buying trips to The Market in High Point, North Carolina. Every April and October it's off to the furnishings wonderland, where he usually shops for three or four days, starting at eight in the morning, stopping around eight at night. After I'd been working as his assistant for 2^{1}/$_{2}$ years, he took me along on the trip to High Point in October of 2001.

Besides the gigantic main building where there are floors and floors of vendors, there are individual showrooms located in temporary buildings that stretch for blocks. Beau rarely uses the shuttle service—he prefers to walk. And he likes the fact that almost every showroom offers food. We were treated to meals for the entire four days by vendors hoping that a good meal would mean good sales.

Beau's accountant had given us a budget. We blew it the very first day. Beau finds a budget as irritating as a mosquito. He knows how many big jobs are on the schedule, knows his clients, and knows how much he must buy to keep the inventory fresh, eclectic, well-stocked, and guaranteed to draw sighs of pleasure from patrons roaming the rooms of the gallery.

In all my interior designing experience, I never have seen a company that operates like the Brownstone Gallery. Never saw the volume of merchandise that comes in and goes out of here. Never saw a clientele list to match Beau's, never saw so many clients who are also his friends.

When I work with Beau, I'm a sponge. Got to be. The man has so much knowledge about his craft, his merchandise, the way to work with clients, that the smartest course for me is to soak it up.

—Joanne Laitkep

The Brownstone Gallery... original one-of-a-kind pieces

ARCHITECTURAL DIGEST
THE INTERNATIONAL MAGAZINE OF FINE INTERIOR DESIGN   MAY/JUNE 1976 $2.95

Architectural Digest Previews: A New Designer

By Gay Elliott McFarland

Several months ago we visited Houston on a scouting trip and lunched at a delightful restaurant/antiques shop, The Brownstone. The décor was so well done that when we met one of the owners, Beau Theriot, we asked to see his home. The next day we visited the Rococo fantasy that marks this young designer's first appearance in a national magazine. . . . beyond the quiet exterior is a visual barrage of furnishings and art objects that delights and somewhat overwhelms the eye. It is an interior with a myriad of antiques, textures, color and architectural usages. The creative use of all these different elements makes the house unique. It is a house that broods, seduces, beckons. Precisely those effects Mr. Theriot wanted. . . . Not yet thirty, Mr. Theriot's future is at least as big as Texas. We look forward to the unfolding of his career.

—Excerpts from the
May/June, 1976, issue of
Architectural Digest

*The Brownstone Gallery . . .
the unusual . . .
the unique*

Completing the process of recruitment, Beau enlisted laborers, sales staff, payroll staff, people with construction ability —including an elite force of master craftsmen—design assistants, upholsterers, someone who could hang a chandelier, and someone else who could drive a nail. With army on board, with inventory in place and ready to dazzle, and with a "creative genius" (commendation courtesy of fellow Houston antique dealer John Holt) positioned at the helm, Beau had established his design base.

Fully staffed and fully equipped, The Brownstone Gallery was strategically positioned as a comprehensive in-house operation that could do it all. With the standard set, the business went forward with a fluency of purpose.

Vision Quest

The process begins with a talking session. Whether by phone, in his office at the gallery, or on site, vision comes quickly to Beau. The design project could be at the architectural drawing phase, could have progressed to slab and dry wall, could even be a long-lived-in home packed to the rafters with a client's existing possessions; no matter what stage of development, once Beau visits the space, he begins to "see."

His ability to bring substance to a dream is startling in its range and particulars. Stand back when Beau begins to conjure imaginatively; as if by divine intervention, magical things will happen—magical for the unimagined innovation. Yet even magic must come down to earth at times, and even the best laid plans of Beau and his men will be accompanied by the very real sound of sledgehammer and buzz saw. It is not unheard of for the first wise decree to be: "Knock out a wall."

Ceilings are often raised and always painted, flying buttresses are flown aloft, and shelving may be installed twenty feet above an entry door to hold a marble statue of Diana at the hunt or Zeus in repose. Where corners are squared, he throws a curve. Where no thought has been given to erecting a column, he will set a stand of columns. Anticipating the placement of a three tiered chandelier over a sunken tub, he will order rewiring. For a staircase railing, there may be wrought iron grapevines intermingled with casts of birds.

Once the job begins to take shape architecturally, it is back to the Brownstone for fabric selection, for color preferences, for discussion of the client's likes and dislikes, for fixtures and furniture, for the creation of stone and wood floor patterns, for carved marble around the fireplace.

If one advances confidently in the direction of his dreams, and endeavors to live the life which he has imagined, he will meet with success unexpected in common hours.

—Henry David Thoreau

Beau's home in River Oaks

> *Life without industry is guilt, and industry without art is brutality.*
>
> —John Ruskin

Then, he imparts instruction to the coalition of artists and artisans in his employ. All the client needs to do is sit back and watch puffs of dreamy hopes and wishes coalesce into a tangible reality.

Ace upholsterer, furniture craftsman, and twenty-five-year Brownstone Gallery veteran Romolo De Los Santos remembers some early rallying words when the army was first being formed. "Beau said he wanted our team to have the capability to do anything and everything—so that's just what we did." Explaining that the "everything" was not limited to the aesthetics, Romolo recalled that in the early years everyone, including Beau, was a "gopher."

"We would go for this, go for that, go for every detail of the job ourselves. We would do the cleaning ourselves, from tapestry to toilets. We would do the labor, do the hauling and the installation, make the beds—not just the construction of beds, but tuck in the sheets and fluff the pillows.

"Beau is a great supporter of the precept that to reach the top, you must start at the bottom. He would say: 'If you start at the top, only way to go is down.'

"What has kept all of us who work with him feeling young and invigorated and crazy about the job is that you never know what's going to happen next. Life with Beau travels miles beyond just being exciting. Our experiences have never been boring, are never repetitious, and we've met some very wonderful people along the way.

"Make a customer happy, and we have that customer for life—and all of their offspring too! The telephone number at the gallery has been handed down from generation to generation as a treasured family heirloom."

Imagine the scene: with four phone lines ringing, assistant Joanne Laitkep is on a call to the stone carver, sister Dianne Maspero is on the phone with the accountant, associate designer Wes Satterwhite is showing customers around the gallery, Virginia Ramsey is taking inventory, and two guys have stopped by to offer Beau a couple of Persian rugs at a bargain price. Big Mike is moving a Louis Quatorze table from here to there, Little Mike is up a ladder taking down a broken chandelier, Romolo wants a decision on wall fabric, J. T. tries to maneuver an oversized museum-framed work of art through the gathered throng.

Carmen arrives with pineapple-mango slushies for everyone, Señor the Chihuahua is napping in his daybed, and Beau and Karol Barnhart are seated at the conference table discussing the details of the bell tower planned for the Barnhart ranch project in Westhof, Texas.

Amid the hustle and bustle, the discussion between Karol and Beau is delivered in a sort of rapid-fire code. It is a conversational shorthand made of stops and starts, sentence fragments, enigmas, conundrums, exclamations, telepathy.

While nonsensical to the uninitiated, these two veterans of the Brownstone campaign understand each other perfectly. At conclusion of their meeting, Beau and Karol look across the table and smile warmly, more than satisfied that strategy has been planned in full, decisions have been made.

Tablescape of Beau's love of the unusual

The following curious exchange between two seasoned soldiers of the decorating wars was transcribed verbatim from a tape recording.

Beau: . . . take a number . . . where's the book . . . put that there.

Karol: . . . made in Quadalajara . . . ideas come like killer bees.

Beau: . . . paint it, rub it down, rub until it looks old . . . Mexico can't touch Brazil.

Karol: . . . colors, getting nervous.

Beau: . . . you nervous . . . turn it all over to me . . . plane's going when.

Karol: . . . pinky-fuchsia cantera.

Beau: . . . spread around porch, different aspect . . . remember the walls.

Karol: . . . woman's privilege to change her mind.

Beau: . . . who knows better than me about that.

Karol: . . . mission white outside.

Beau: . . . found in all these years, if it looks good on one piece, the whole will be fabulous . . . grass, trees, sky, sun, moon . . . in the long run, so much better.

Karol: . . . you're reassuring.

Beau: . . . I want to be involved in every commode.

Karol: . . . we need to turn the stone man loose.

Beau: . . . get Ruben on the phone for me please . . . don't like those rounded columns . . . big carved mirror at the entrance, get the feeling of expanse . . . hacienda.

Karol: . . . the old chest here.

Beau: . . . that doesn't bother me.

Karol: . . . save the marriage, whole family . . . many views.

Beau: . . . bougainvillea all around . . . he's got me on hold.

Karol: . . . Kim said in San Antonio.

Beau: . . . you and Kim, pretty women.

Karol: . . . want to open the window, walk out of the dining room.

Beau: . . . can't spend all my budget on stonework, the stuff's not cheap . . . let me make decisions . . . come, Señor.

Karol: . . . Ruben will do windows.

Beau: . . . don't want to duplicate the fireplaces.

Karol: . . . not trying to do a pure mission home . . . who wants anything pure.

Beau: . . . no rugs today, thank you.

Karol: . . . open shelves or everything closed.

Beau: . . . all doors.

Karol: . . . with twenty-foot ceilings, how do we change the lightbulbs?

Beau: . . . Joanne, get your notebook out . . . tall ladders.

With twenty-foot ceilings,
how do we change the lightbulbs?

—Karol Barnhart

Karol: . . . do you think my husband would tear a picture out of a magazine and say "Look, oh how pretty!" . . . not in a million years.

Beau: . . . mossy, green sage.

Karol: . . . not sure . . . not sure.

Beau: . . . take it home, throw it over a sofa, live with it.

Karol: . . . when tiles come, go out to ranch, draw them a picture, stick it on the bathroom wall.

Beau: . . . you want a bowl of soup.

Karol: . . . jackrabbits.

The Decorating Wars: Joanne, Karol, Wes, and Beau with Señor refereeing

The Galanos dream home in Chappell Hill, Texas

Karol and Beau's "conversation" represents a work in progress. The following interview with Donna and Peter Galanos describes the wrap-up of a successful project. October of the new millennium found Donna and Peter waving goodbye to the cramped trailer they had lived in during the eighteen-month construction of their dream home. A handsome residence overlooking the countryside near Chappell Hill, Texas, the well-proportioned structure is set like a crown jewel at the center of the Galanos horse farm.

Located a mile west of Highway 290—the road Beau religiously travels two times a week, going from Austin to Houston and back again—the farm was a regular stopover for Beau when he was engaged in the duties of design consultant and interior decorator. With the job completed, he continues to make side trips to visit the Galanos family. "But, now he comes for supper," says Peter.

LEFT OVERLEAF: *Residence of Ann and Travis Traylor*

102

Interior Motive

Q: *It took years for Donna to drag you into the Brownstone Gallery, Peter. Among all of Beau's clients, Donna wins the prize for most tenacious interior motive.*

Peter: Seven years to be exact. Donna had talked about Beau for seven years before we made an appointment to see him. Once there, I paced around the gallery; I was uncomfortable, wanted the ordeal over with. Knowing what I know now, I came close to making the biggest mistake of my life.

Donna: During that first interview, sensing Peter's reluctance, I thought all was lost. Then Beau said, "Proportion is everything in a house," and I relaxed. Symmetry, proportion—these are magic words when you want my husband's attention.

Peter: Thank goodness, before the architectural plan was finalized, Beau was on the job. He massaged the drawings, had great new ideas for construction. His input gave us the creative edge from that point forward. An amazing interior designer certainly, but our project benefited by tapping into his other talents too.

Q: *Someone once said there must be hundreds of rooms in Beau's head, all spinning with beautiful visions.*

Peter: All you have to do is walk into the gallery to know that's true. Donna and I shopped many stores, even the Dallas Market, but the merchandise left us cold. But, once inside the Brownstone, we wanted to buy half the things in there. Every piece in our house came from the gallery. We had one problem though. We would tag things that we loved, tape the *Sold* banner solidly on them; then when we returned to the gallery in a month or so, Beau would have a beautiful new shipment in. I began to wish we had two houses to decorate.

Q: *Did you ever disagree with one of his suggestions? Was there any time during the construction or design process when doubt raised its ugly head?*

Donna: Yes, once. Beau stopped by for a quick visit on his way to Austin. Wasn't in the house more than five minutes. In that five minutes, he taped a swatch of red cloth to the wall in the dining room. When Beau left, Peter and I stood staring at the cloth in horror.

Dear Beau: It's 2:53 A.M., and I should be in bed, but I'm too excited to sleep! I know you have worked on bigger houses with bigger budgets, and this is one of your smaller jobs. Still, I wanted you to know that Peter and I feel so appreciative, so blessed that our dream home was created by a man of peerless honesty and integrity, a man so generous with his time, so generous with his tremendous talent. On Friday, when the job is completed and you and J. T. drive out of the driveway, the two people waving goodbye care about you deeply and thank you for making us the happiest family in the world.

—Donna Galanos

> *To win the interest of sophisticated clientele, you must fascinate them with sophisticated planning.*
>
> —Beau Theriot

Peter: When that swatch went up, he almost lost us. We stammered, walked around the house for a couple of weeks agonizing, we looked at that wild red color and couldn't handle it.

Donna: We were nervous wrecks, but we didn't say anything about it to Beau; we didn't want to hurt his feelings. We decided to keep our mouths shut and our fingers crossed.

Peter: Happy ending to the story, just as I imagine there are happy endings to all Beau stories. Work proceeded, and the dining room turned out better than wonderful—rich and beautiful and dramatic. We are definitely red dining room people now. Can't help loving that room, can't help loving him.

Donna: I told Beau that he knows better about what we like than we do.

Q: *After 18 months, bet you were glad when the day came to move out of the trailer home and into your wonderful new house. Beau is legendary for his one-day installations. This is a big house—at completion of what had to be a major installation, is the legend still alive?*

Donna: First let me describe the night before. The painters finished at 6:00 P.M., and the carpet people showed up at 6:30. At 9:00, the cleaning crew arrived. The carpet installation was completed by midnight, which meant the cleaning crew had to work until around 1:30 A.M. When they left, I began leaning paintings against the wall for Beau to hang, while Peter dragged our mattress into the Great Room so we could spend our first night inside our new house. We finally closed our eyes at 3:00 A.M.

Peter: Exactly six hours later Beau arrived—Beau, a couple of 18-wheelers, and a crew of twelve workers. We stood and watched them unload our beautiful furniture, furniture we hadn't seen in a year and a half. It felt like Christmas.

Donna: Then Santa's elves went to work. One woman was dusting, another making the beds, one person was hanging drapes, another putting down rugs, someone was wiping mirrors, another person was hanging artwork, another hanging chandeliers, and one guy's job was to put bulbs in the lamps. Beau brought in plants and flowers, arranged the knickknacks and accessories on tables and in bookcases. Everybody had a job, everyone was busy.

Peter: And Beau orchestrated the whole show. It was like he truly was conducting a symphony. All of the players were synchronized, all knew their parts, and he was on the podium, baton in the air, creating the loveliest music.

Donna and Peter Galanos

Donna: Peter and I were speechless. I had to go out to the trailer and just sit there, taking deep breaths. It's pretty overwhelming to see a dream come true.

Peter: By 5:30 in the afternoon, it was done. We had gone from a totally empty house to a place that should be photographed by *Architectural Digest*. Beau had created magic for us. It looked like we had lived here forever. I can happily report that the legend is alive and kicking.

Donna: The legend is also a teaser. At 5:30, when the trucks rolled away, Beau came in and said: "When's the party?" I asked: "What party?" Beau reminded me that he'd promised the house would be ready for a party by sunset. Wish now that I'd invited everyone we know over for dinner.

Peter: My favorite story is about what our son, Alex, said when he came home from school. His eyes were wide as we walked with him through the finished house. He was very quiet, thinking hard. Finally he asked if it would be okay if he lived in this house instead of the trailer. It felt good to say: "This is your home now, Alex."

Beau orchestrated the whole show. It was like he truly was conducting a symphony. All of the players were synchronized, all knew their parts, and he was on the podium, baton in the air, creating the loveliest music.

—Peter Galanos

Beau's Army

Beau said he wanted our team to have the capability to do anything and everything—so that's just what we did. Make a customer happy, and we have that customer for life—and all of their offspring too! The telephone number at the gallery has been handed down from generation to generation as a treasured family heirloom.

—Romolo De Los Santos

'96 4 1

Major installation in the home of Tova and Ace Kindred

I like to think of the excellent employees working at the gallery as Beau's army. Marines of the moving day installation. These are some tough, talented, well-trained people.

—Karol Barnhart

The Oasis
PLACEMENT OF THE SUN

OASIS CANTINA DEL LAGO

In 1979, Beau paid a cool million five for a 500-acre tract that drifts along a bluff overlooking Austin's Lake Travis. Without having any particular plan in mind about how to develop the land, he based the impetus solely on the beauty of the setting. He loved the hills formed of limestone and bedrock and a terrain as welcoming to cacti as bougainvillea, and he found great attraction in a natural wilderness rolling high and pristine through some really fine Texas air.

> *Wouldn't it be neat to have a little restaurant over there on that hill?*
>
> —Beau Theriot

But what finally sold him was the sunset. Standing at the land's edge, gazing down at a march of trees waning into an ever-deepening green, glancing up at day's end across a lake radiantly lit with an impossible kaleidoscope of colors, he beheld a vista that looked good enough to eat.

A future dream would suggest what to do with the land, and what to do with the little ramshackle ranch house, which was the only structure on the property. Putting the current dream in motion, Beau bought the tract and let imaginings for development simmer awhile. By 1982, with modest renovation on the ranch house completed, Beau opened a modest little eatery, total seating capacity—300. The initial plan was to feed hamburgers and beer to sunburned patrons who stopped in after spending the day at the lake.

But never a man to rest on one laurel, Beau revved up the dream machine once again and thought of bigger things. As past performance in other ventures had clearly shown, when ideas come to Beau, they grow. To create a spectacular centerpiece for his land, he expanded on the original structure and began decking down the side of a 450-foot slope in a multileveled configuration designed to give all visitors a clear view of that delicious sunset.

Beau built a crazy-legged tree house—a decked protuberance jutting out from the hillside that, at last count, is comprised of forty planked landings capable of seating 2,000. Whether the drink called for is a Perfect Margarita—signature quaff of the establishment—or a tall Coke, there are five bar stations to answer drink requests.

Evening at The Oasis

Furnished with six to twenty tables per deck, each deck is fitted out with white plastic chairs, tilted umbrellas, natural wood railings, and a series of stairsteps that connect the giant complex. During the high season, the employment roster lists 275 waiters, waitresses, bartenders, managers, and kitchen staff. To organize service at The Oasis, it is necessary for those directing food and bar service traffic to wear headphones. The operation could be compared to running a cruise ship, only this ship sails on the tops of trees.

Appearing at the restaurant nightly, the sunset receives star billing. Ringing the sunset bell is a treat for guests, and when the bell tolls, signaling the sun's final glorious plunge into the lake, the sun is given a standing ovation. An annual competition that brings shutterbugs out from their darkrooms to the decks of The Oasis has long been the standard for the best in sunset photography; and when prizes are awarded, winners find that sun-worshipping has its rewards.

Though heralded as the largest restaurant in Texas (and perhaps the world), The Oasis Cantina del Lago continues to be a work in progress. Because Beau is a builder, someone who thinks in layers, he is not one who will ever be resigned to the statement: "It is finished."

There came a night some years ago, when the sun had disappeared and the hour was a little past seven, that he said to himself: "Now what?" Beau looked around, saw a thousand people in heightened spirits and festive moods, and decided it would be a good idea to put in a dance floor, hire some terrific bands, and offer his guests an after-sunset, but equally celestial, place to continue the party. He would give them, if not the music of the spheres, then music of Rotel & The Hot Tomatoes—a group destined to become a favorite show band at The Oasis.

The sunsets make The Oasis the best show in town.

I am the magical mouse
I don't eat cheese
I eat sunsets
And the tops of trees.

—Kenneth Patchen

Regulars know that on weekends it is difficult to find a parking spot along Comanche Trail, the road that curves across the mountaintop. A crowd-pleasing success from the start, the open-air dance pavilion, Starlight Terrace, draws families and college students, tourists and terpsichoreans to the dance on Friday and Saturday nights. And on Sundays, it has become an Oasis tradition to offer step-by-step instruction in Latin dances—merengue, samba, or a saucy salsa.

Keeping to a Proustian line of thinking that "the cure for dreamers is not to dream less but to dream more, to dream all the time," Beau saw his dream grow to be as big as all outdoors. And it was in the outdoors that he next established a world-class sculpture garden that features a collection of bronze statues ranging from the whimsical to museum-quality works of art.

The Oasis naturally became a one-of-a-kind destination spot, sought out by visitors from around the world. The gigantic tree house restaurant above a pretty lake invites the world to an experience of art and music, dancing, shopping, games, stage shows, and, of course, it is recognized as "the sunset capital of Texas." In The Oasis guestbook are countless entries from people who have visited from all fifty states and from more than forty countries across the world.

Something's always brewing at The Oasis.

What's happening at the Starlight Terrace, the live music venue at The Oasis

The restaurant has been honored consistently over the years with awards of varying tribute. A few notables include: "Best Place to Impress Out-of-Towners," "Best Place to Drink Outdoors," "Best Restaurant With a View," "One of the 7 Wonders of Austin," "Texas Top 10 Tourist Attractions."

But the irrepressible innovator is not through yet. A recently constructed three-story tower next to the restaurant was designed

specifically to meet requests from patrons for a private party venue at The Oasis. The grand salon, christened Top of the Oasis, is located on the third floor, overlooking the lake. It is served by a new state-of-the-art kitchen, and has room to spare for dancing the Viennese waltz while entertaining 200 at a formal dinner.

The latest development, located just across the road from The Oasis, is Beau's most ambitious addition to the complex to date: The Treasury is a 15,000-square-foot shopping mecca for antiques, collectibles, art, and furnishings of merit selected by the master. Housed on the third floor of The Treasury is an eclectic display of Beau's private art collection. Fortunate are the art lovers in the crowd who might be given a guided tour by the collector himself. It does not take much to be invited to share the wonders of Beau's world. Reward him with a smile, a spark of interest, and you're in.

The story of The Oasis is best told in the words of Beau's brother Joe. The youngest of the Theriot siblings, Joe Theriot was born seven years and three days after big brother Beau. His official natal day was September 4, but it wasn't until his thirteenth year that Joe found out he did not share the same birth date with brother Beau. It was Joe's understanding that he and Beau were born on the same day, September 1, which is, in fact, the legitimate date marking Beau's entrance into the world. But for Joe, time was switched at birth.

Beau and Joe at The Oasis

Bureaucratic circumstance compelled their mother Nadine to alter Joe's birth certificate. She justified tinkering with his natural horoscope by putting blame on the Port Arthur school system, the first of September being the cut-off date for enrollment.

Joe recalls that for the first thirteen years of his life, Nadine always baked an oversized sheet cake—one half was inscribed "Happy Birthday Bobby"; the other side read "Happy Birthday, Joe." "Today," Joe says with a sigh of satisfaction, "Today I get a whole cake of my own."

In 1983 Joe, his wife Mary, and their children moved to Austin so that Joe could assist Beau with management of The Oasis. In operation only for one year at that time, The Oasis was a ramshackle ranch house fitted out with picnic tables and sporting only a single deck. If making the long drive west of the city to visit the unprepossessing spot on the hill seemed the right thing to do, a customer got a rather limited menu for the effort—hamburger and a beer, hot dog and a Coke.

"And they got to see a pretty spectacular sunset over the lake," says Joe. "We always had the sunset."

Above: Dancing at The Oasis . . . always a happening
Right: Beau and Nadine at The Oasis' 20th anniversary party, June 2002

We were throwing around ideas for naming the place. I came up with "The Chameleon." They all stared at me. Finally Beau said, "Liz, that's a lizard." And my very good friend, Beau's sister Dianne, was quick to add, "Besides, how would you find 'Chameleon' in the telephone book? Nobody can spell it." I was able to redeem myself a few years later when Beau wanted a good logo caption for The Oasis. When I dubbed it The Sunset Capital of Texas, I made up for the lizard.

—Liz Cook

119

BUILDING FROM THE TOP DOWN

A Remembrance by Joe Theriot

Brother Joe

For him there are no boundaries . . .

I'm in awe of Beau's creativity, and have been since childhood. Never met anybody as committed to proceeding with original thought—no matter what the project—as my brother. He doesn't think linearly, doesn't think laterally, doesn't even think bilaterally. Beau thinks differently. For him, there are no boundaries, no barriers, no limits. And most interesting of all—even Webster's would have trouble defining his particular brand of imagination.

I always wished that I could think like that, but I analyze the hell out of everything and spend all of my creative efforts on figuring fifty reasons why an idea won't work.

My favorite Beau quote goes to the heart of his singularity—and it's something I've heard him express often—"I have to try," my brother always says. "I know you think I'm crazy, but I have to try."

He's fearless. When you consider the hurdles that had to be jumped, the Herculean labors that had to be endured, the many challenges that tried to stop completion of The Oasis, then any normal guy, watching from the sidelines, would say: "Hey, when did Superman decide to go into the restaurant business?"

To bring The Oasis to the status it now holds—prominently hailed as a Texas landmark—required superhuman patience and perseverance. Development of The Oasis was like a voyage, requiring the captain at the helm to sail into unknown waters. On the horizon there were sea monsters—their evil little heads popped up with regularity. Beau slew them all, and we sailed on.

Never met anybody as committed to proceeding with original thought — no matter what the project — as my brother .... Beau thinks differently.

In its original incarnation, the mountain had been a working ranch; and, during the early years of the restaurant, there was only one access road for people wanting to get down to or up from the lake. Comanche Trail Ranch—a sweeping expanse of mesquite, cypress, and cacti—overlooks a portion of the lake called the Main Sailing Basin, and is a favored recreation area on a waterway that drifts along for sixty-four miles.

Beau's original idea for The Oasis could not be described as complex. Actually, it was the essence of simplicity. He wanted to open a small biergarten, serve Tex-Mex and hamburgers, be the informal joint at the top of the mountain that welcomed folks wearing bathing suits and flip-flops.

About the design, the construction—no architects were involved. My brother would sketch his plan on a sheet of paper, tack it up on a wall, and say: "This is what I want." The head bartender back in the early years was also a master carpenter. I had some proficiency with hammer and nails myself, so I served as carpenter's assistant. We would come in early in the morning, build decks, make repairs, then go home, shower and change, and be back to open the restaurant at 4:00 P.M. In those days, The Oasis was only open for dinner.

Eventually, other employees helped out with construction. Some of the other bartenders pitched in, as well as college kids from UT and Austin Community College who also worked as waiters and waitresses, and we did hire a few day laborers—but none of us could really be considered members of a professional construction crew.

In the beginning, we were feeding around 300 people a day on the weekends. We had this dinky little kitchen, a couple of bar stations, very limited inside seating (which caused problems on stormy nights), no live music. The parking lot wasn't paved, and cars kicked up a lot of dust. Our clientele ran from leather-encased bikers to carloads of moms, dads, kids, and dogs or from grandpa and grandma out for a Sunday drive to college students who stopped in after spending the day at Hippie Hollow (a cove on Lake Travis down the hill from The Oasis, unofficially designated as a nude beach, where to swim in a swimsuit or to swim without a swimsuit is left to personal discretion).

Building from the top down

Expansion was a never-ending project. It seemed that the more decks we had, the more decks we needed. Yet, even as we added on, nobody—except maybe Beau—ever imagined a multi-decked configuration constituting forty separate levels. Forty separate levels that would seat 2,000, and with each of those 2,000 chairs guaranteed an unobstructed view of the sunset. As we grew, the concept changed. We ceased being a wet bathing suit joint very early on.

An interesting thing to know is that Beau did not buy 500 acres at the top of Comanche Trail Ranch because he thought the drive-by traffic would provide a profitable business. The real inspiration behind the purchase is more Beau-esque. In translation, Beau-esque means the direct opposite of crass commercialism. His decision to buy the acreage speaks volumes, and demonstrates the fact that Beau thinks differently from the rest of us. The reason he wanted to acquire the dilapidated ranch house and the surrounding wilderness is best expressed in Beau's own words. "I've been all over the world—I've visited some gorgeous spots. But this place wins my vote as one of the loveliest I've ever seen—imagine finding this view in Texas!"

Hanging Out

Not everybody was glad to see The Oasis open for business. Our right to exist was challenged repeatedly, by nay-saying official types as well as by our neighbors. We had to swat off the slings and arrows of outrageous building and property code requirements, and we had to defend our case, more than once, before the Comanche Trail Homeowners Association. As we grew, as more guests started to fill up the decks, the tranquil birdsong that once dominated that remote area was enhanced with some really fine live band music. Those rhythmic tunes wafted out over the lake for miles, and apparently wafted into some lake homes where music lovers did not reside.

To pacify the homeowners association, Beau offered a compromise. The Oasis could keep the live music, but we agreed to turn the amplifiers away from the lake, and into the interior of the restaurant. And we agreed to cut off the music by 10:30 P.M., which was okay with us since The Oasis has never been, and was never intended to be, a wee-small-hours-of-the-morning spot.

More than anything else, The Oasis was built in tribute to the sunset. Our primary modus operandi is to offer a daily celebration of the sunset. From day one, we concentrated our attention—and the attention of our guests—on that glorious, slow descent of the sun.

As time went on, perception of The Oasis in the public mind changed. We were no longer regarded as simply the hamburger joint above the lake. The addition of gift shop, sculpture garden, a game room for kids—combined with the magnificent view, courteous and efficient service, and a picturesque setting where stair-stepping decks were festooned with brightly colored umbrellas—won us the reputation as one of the best tourist attractions in Texas.

It was Beau's original concept to construct a giant tree house. One that seemed to defy gravity, hanging down from the mountain top on spidery wooden legs, jutting out over the lake as if plans for its construction had been formulated on a kid's erector set rather than an architect's drafting table.

Charming to me, and to the entire Theriot family, was the occasion a few years ago when Beau was presented with an award from the Texas Lumbermen's Association for the creative use of natural wood in both construction and in retention of the original trees on the property. The award was especially meaningful to the family because both our father and our grandfather worked in the lumber business.

Beau saved the trees for shade and for beauty, and when you see them growing right up through the decking, and billowing out in lovely greenery straight down the hillside, the impression is of floating on top of the forest.

The sunset is only one of the attractions at The Oasis.

In the eleven years that I managed The Oasis, incidents of the bizarre were rare. However, there are some interesting stories . . .

The Longhorn Bar is below the main indoor dining room. Off the bar, decks jut out on the hillside, and under the decks there is a room for the ice machines. (Ice has always been of high priority: at The Oasis you can never have enough ice.) Anyway, one hot summer day, the bartender went into the ice room and came right back out again, his eyes bugging. "There's a naked guy in the ice room," the bartender informed us.

The manager at the time was the eminently capable Colleen. Colleen said: "I'll see about this! Stand aside," and she entered the ice room, shutting the door firmly behind her. After awhile, she emerged again and related The Sad Story of the Drifted Hippie.

The tale of the fellow's exposed tail began when he arrived at The Oasis by climbing straight up the hillside from the lake below. The victim of bad planning, he had set out on an inflated raft from Hippie Hollow. Dressed in the altogether, wearing nothing but a smile, he was soon lulled into peaceful sleep by the easy rocking of the raft upon the

124

water. The journey progressed in true libertarian fashion—free-willed, laid-back, without direction. While he slept, however, the raft had drifted far beyond the parameters allocated to the bare-bottomed cavorting of the Hollow people.

Finding himself suddenly gasping for breath and splashing around in the lake, the man discovered that all the air had gone out of his raft. It was a rude awakening. He then had to make a choice. Either scramble over sharp-edged rocks, scrub brush, scorpions, and other impediments along the shoreline to return to the distant Hippie Hollow, or make the short climb up to The Oasis. Decision made, the fellow climbed up to the restaurant and hid himself behind an ice machine, where he had shivered for hours, friendless and alone. After delivering a brief lecture on proper public decorum, the venerable Colleen borrowed a pair of shorts from a busboy and told the hippie to cover his losses and go home.

Water, Water Everywhere, Nor Any Drop To Drink

Like the plot line for the movie *Chinatown,* our biggest concern for many years was water. The lack of it. Neither Comanche Trail Ranch nor any region on the mountain received city water; and back in the 1980s no one seemed in a hurry to correct the situation. Storage at The Oasis was limited to two 6,000-gallon tanks. The County would haul water out to us and fill the tanks. Usually the water supply was, if not plentiful, then at least adequate to the demands of the weekend crowds.

One morning Beau and I sat down with a slick-talking peddler who threw us a sales pitch about a new water treatment system that he guaranteed would enable us to be self-sufficient. We would never again have to rely on the city, or on the county, for our water. Way it worked seemed simple enough. We would take the water from the lake, treat it ourselves, and an endless supply of the precious stuff would be ours forever. We bought the system.

The next visitor to the office was an inspector from the Health Department. The guy wasted no time in pleasantries. He got straight to the point. "This system is not approved," he told us. "You will have to go back to having water hauled in."

A Margarita and the sunset make a winning combination at The Oasis.

The Oasis Sunset

1 ounce Bacardi Limon
1 ounce Captain Morgan's Spiced Rum
6 ounces lemonade
3 ounces orange juice
splash of grenadine
1/2 ounce Bacardi 151

Combine the Bacardi Limon and Spiced Rum in a large hurricane glass. Fill the glass with chipped ice and add the lemonade, orange juice and grenadine, stirring to mix well. Add the Bacardi 151 very slowly, allowing it to float on the surface. Serve with a festive cocktail umbrella.

The unceasing expansion at The Oasis soon resulted in the hard fact that we had outgrown our tank capacity. It was catastrophic to a restaurant that needs to fill 1,500 water glasses while, at the same time, accommodating an equal amount of flushes.

We decided to make friends with the guys at the local fire station. Friendship secured, we made them a deal. If they would bring their trucks over and fill up our tanks, we would make generous donations to the fire department. That worked pretty well for awhile. Only cessation of service was when the firemen were called away to put out a fire somewhere. Nice relationship, but somewhat undependable.

I remember one weekend when we were so desperate we called a bottled water company—Oasis Water, oddly enough—and placed a rush order for a truckload of 5-gallon jugs to be sent over immediately. When the truck arrived, employees were positioned to off-load those jugs of designer water and heave them along a chain gang up to the roof above the kitchen. As fast as that very expensive water was received, it was dumped through a hole in the roof down to a collection vat.

I learned something very interesting that night. Every time a commode is flushed, three gallons of water goes down the drain. We were fighting a losing battle. By 8:00, we were out of designer water and had to close down. Beau and I sat up on the roof reflecting on life, liberty, and the pursuit of moisture. We were at a crisis point. Something had to be done. There in the moonlight, with my brother at my side, I decided to become a candidate. I would place my name on the ballot and run for a position on the water board.

I didn't win the election, but was able to make some noise, shake things up a bit. After petitioning the water board to include The Oasis in the water district, approval was granted, and they allowed us to run our own water line—a line to be used strictly by The Oasis. Hallelujah. And then we moved on to the sewage system.

Naturally neither city nor county facilitated our need to dispose of waste. Just as we outgrew tank capacity for storing water, we discovered that all those flushing commodes required an area of processing that extended far beyond our existing septic field. One hundred and twenty-five thousand dollars later, we had a new septic field. Ever the entrepreneur, ever the creative thinker, Beau decided to plant a vineyard directly below the super expansion of the new purification treatment plant.

The new and improved, and very expensive, septic field that processes effluvium et al from The Oasis comes with a solid gold guarantee that the water nurturing the tender vines in Beau's vineyard will produce grapes of a most distinctive quality. I can hardly wait for the first tasting of The Oasis vintage.

And, as always, I remain fascinated to see what my brother will be up to next.

The Beau Experience
SPACES WITH VIEWPOINTS AND
CHARMING STORIES

BEAU GESTE

"No one has ever accused me of following the crowd," said Beau in response to a question about the creative process involved in his design methodology. The reverse is true, however, when considering the hundreds of clients for whom he has produced interiors of distinction over the years. The crowd has certainly followed Beau. Followed with a happy, snappy spring to the step. There is a reason.

Love makes one more calm about many things, and so one is more fit for one's work.

—Vincent Van Gogh

Anyone who has worked with a decorator can testify to what often happens when an artistic temperament enters the cozy confines of one's home and hearth. When clashes and holocausts occur between client and designer, the work might reach completion but the contenders rarely wind up as friends. Putting a value on friendship that far exceeds any monetary gain, Beau would rather hug you than slug you. Fit for work and ready for love: that's the Beau Experience in a nutshell.

Naturally, this brings an element of comfort to the working relationship. Beau's world spins on the axis of amicability, and to keep a friend is always on his mind, personally and professionally. A clue to the degree of his artistic temperament is revealed in his stated philosophy regarding interior decorating: "Every detail of the design is meant to promote comfort, a sense of beauty, a mood of romance, an appreciation of classicism, and a relaxed response to the environment."

These details are frequently very innovative. In the first house Beau decorated for Janeen Fertitta, he decided the best thing to do would be to put black silk on the walls in the entry hall. About the effect, Janeen said: "My foyer looked like it was all dressed up in a shiny tuxedo."

To create a showstopper for Janeen's beach house, Beau made a shopping trip to Mexico where he found colorful fish encased in glass bubbles. Interspersing the bubble fish along an iron railing constructed to resemble waves, he created a one-of-a-kind staircase.

The charming library of Fredell and Bobby Deutser

ABOVE: *The cozy great room of the Traylor's retreat in Beaver Creek, Colorado*
RIGHT OVERLEAF: *The dining room of the Traylor residence in Houston*

By overscaling I achieve the feeling of a larger home.

—Beau Theriot

And when Janeen and her husband Julian Fertitta moved into their new home in Stablewood in 1999, Beau decided to illuminate the outside terrace with a grand chandelier that would be bordered by drapery billowing down as elegantly as drapes hung in a formal dining room. "Beau and umbrella fabric," explained Janeen, "gave us the most dramatic outdoor patio in town!"

These are only a few of the innovative touches achieved in a successful three-project collaboration. In fact, the projects proved so successful that when Janeen's mother, Esther Smith, and sister, Gwen Irwin, acquired new homes in the beautiful Glen Lakes compound in Dallas, they also placed decorating duties in the hands of the talented designer. In one sweet swoop, design assignments for three of his favorite ladies required the Beau touch.

All In The Family

Q: *Quickly, off the top of your head, an insight into Beau's decorating style.*

Janeen: He sees lots of ways to do something—there's never any wrong, there's just another way to do it.

Esther: Years after a job has been completed, he can still describe every square inch of a client's home. I can call him, say I need this or that, and he brings a piece that is not only harmonious with the décor but the dimensions are also perfect.

Gwen: He doesn't like white ceilings.

Q: *Would you expand on that thought, Gwen.*

Gwen: Walking through the house that my husband Dick and I had recently purchased in Dallas, Beau kept looking up at the ceilings and shaking his head. He said: "Let's get rid of these white ceilings—the glare's blinding creative thought." We had all the ceilings repainted immediately.

Janeen: Beau hates it when you don't do your ceilings. At my house in Farnham Park— the first project we did together—he wanted black marble in the dining room. But you can't stick black marble up on a ceiling, it's too heavy. So Beau found this guy in Dallas who took thin panels of brown pressed wood and painted them to look exactly like blocks of marble. Wonderfully dramatic, what an effect!

Q: *Janeen, you've worked with Beau on three different homes that were different in style. Is there one constant that never changes in his approach to a project?*

Janeen: Yes, the "Ta-dah" effect. Like a magician amazing the audience with what he can pull out of a hat, Beau designs so that no matter which door you open, no matter which room you walk into, the natural reaction is "Ta-dah!" Applause soon follows.

Q: *Esther, the interior of your home gives the pleasing impression of being inside a colorfully blooming flower garden. It's a unique accomplishment that is singular in Beau's design repertoire. Describe the stages of the concept development.*

Esther: I had lost my husband a year before, and Beau—whom I have always thought of as a friend first, decorator second—wanted to do something to cheer me up. Said he wanted to give me a new life, to create a happy house, a home that would inspire delight every waking hour of the day. To begin the process, he put me to work. My assignment was to get a bunch of home decorating magazines and start tearing out pictures of rooms that I liked. In short order, I sent him fifty pages of wonderful photographs, with notes scribbled about colors preferred, fabrics admired, furnishings I especially liked.

Q: *Did you to travel from Dallas to Houston during the planning stage to confer with him?*

Esther: Yes, I would come to Houston to meet Beau and Janeen at the Brownstone Gallery, where Beau had set up vignettes—placements of furniture, light fixtures, artwork, accessories—for us to consider. We would switch this lamp for that lamp, debate over fabrics, move chairs around. Sometimes the decision-making process was difficult for my darling daughter. Janeen has wonderful taste and ideas, and she's not shy about expressing opinion. However, Janeen wanted this to be my project, so she did a lot of tongue-biting.

Janeen: I'd leave the two of them alone and go into another part of the gallery while Mother and Beau worked together. Occasionally I couldn't help myself; I stopped biting my tongue and put my two cents in. Something I learned very early working with Beau is that the more you talk to him about a project— the more expressive you can be with details—the more creative he becomes.

Gwen: The gallery is a candy store for grown-ups who love gorgeous stuff. Just picking out fabric is an exhilarating experience. If I'd been there, the "ohs and ahs" would have been delivered in triplicate.

Q: *Once selection was accomplished, excitement accelerated as you looked forward to delivery day and setup.*

Esther: I remember the house was empty, the rooms were all painted in bright, lovely colors—persimmon, green apple, daffodil yellow, watermelon—wonderful, happy colors (and yes, even the ceilings). I was waiting for Beau to arrive when the developer of Glen Lakes stopped by to say he wanted to meet the owner of "the Easter egg house." Having lived in the same home for forty years—one decorated to accommodate myself, my husband, and the whims of our little girls—my new house was quite a departure. "Easter egg" is an accurate and delightful description.

Q: *So the developer leaves, and here comes Beau.*

Esther: Here comes Beau with four vans full of furniture. All three of my daughters were there to help, as well as my granddaughter, three hired helpers, Beau, and four of his men. Twenty-seven hours later, the house looked like it does today. Every box was emptied and removed, drapes were hung, chandeliers up, rugs down, furniture in place, on the tables were bowls of orchids.

Q: *Even with everyone pitching in, seems like the job was completed in record time. When Beau gets on a roll, he's tireless. What fuels that kind of energy?*

Esther: I'd say barbecue sandwiches. When I asked what I could do to help, he gave me a specific assignment: "Love," he said, "just keep feeding me barbecue sandwiches— just keep them coming." I was running to the barbecue stand night and day.

ABOVE AND RIGHT OVERLEAF: First Fertitta residence, a Georgian in Farnham Park

ABOVE AND RIGHT: Latest Fertitta residence, one of many Beau has designed with friend Janine Fertitta

Gwen: Beau loves our mother. As busy as he is, he calls regularly just to check on her. On one occasion, we were throwing Mother a birthday party and, of course, Beau was invited. His schedule was so tight that he couldn't leave Austin until late, even though he had appointments slated for early the next day. But that didn't stop Beau. He put on his tux, rented a plane, flew to Dallas, came to the party bearing gifts and kisses, then turned around and went home.

Janeen: I haven't met a client yet who did not become his friend.

Q: *Janeen, besides the "ta-dah" effect, have you observed other traits customary to his working style?*

Janeen: The words: "Trust me on this"—a catch phrase that catches the essence of Beau. I like to play a game with him. A game that tests his spatial planning. Over the years I've discovered that his mind thinks in quadrants, and he rarely misses with measurements—even though he uses no instruments to measure. No instruments except his eyes and that formidable brain.

Q: *Will you give an example of how the game is played.*

Janeen: I am a builder, so I understand that careful preplanning must precede house construction to determine where to put floor plugs, wall sconces, painting lights, and so forth. You have to know where to put the electrical boxes before the sheet rock goes up, before the finished floor is installed. That is, most people do. Then here comes Beau. When the base floor is still rough concrete, he'll say: "I want the electrical box $43^1/2$ inches from the finished floor—that would be right about here." And later, when the floor goes in, the sheet rock's up, durn if it's not within an inch—he's never more than an inch off. That's the game. He wins every time.

Q: *Is there a category that describes his decorating style?*

Janeen: There's no name for his style. He's just Beau. There is nothing stiff in his design technique. For example, I have a monkey chandelier in my bathroom. Some of his ideas sound outrageous, then you think about it awhile, and realize what's going on is a whole lot of fun that is meant to give you a whole lot of joy at completion.

Gwen: The way he mixes things is wonderful. He'll put a ten-dollar piece next to a ten thousand–dollar piece. I have this fabulous statue, a work of fine art. Every Christmas holiday, Beau comes over and sticks a red Christmas bulb in my elegant statue's belly button.

Esther: His whimsical side is neatly balanced by his serious side. Like my husband, Beau cannot sit around and loaf. He believes relaxation is not productive. Even when you do catch him taking a breather, that excellent mind is always clicking.

Someone once said that a sense of humor gives us the best sense of what it must be like to hang around with God. If laughter is not the resonating sound preferred and practiced within the halls of Heaven, then we are all monkeys' uncles.

According to his very good friend, Charles Joekel, Beau has a sense of humor equal to his sense of style and his sense of fair play. "All are right up there near perfect," says the gentleman, who is endowed with a heightened sense of humor of his own. Describing himself as an "aging lion," the entrepreneurial Mr. Joekel still, however, strides with the pride in the business world.

In their twenty-five-year association, natural progression led the two friends to become partners on several projects—the collaboration based on mutual respect for each other's business prowess and straight dealing.

Although Mr. Joekel had never before given an interview and expressed deep reservations about talking into a tape recorder, a nice tall vodka rocks quelled apprehension. After a sip or two, the question-answer session proceeded without hitch in the comfort of his exquisitely furnished home.

The Beauty Of The Deal

Q: *Your aquarium is spectacular—fills up the whole wall. Was it Beau's idea to put an aquarium opposite the dining area?*

Charles: No, Beau watched it being built with dismay. But I've been raising fish ever since my son was five, and that was thirty years ago. When I had the 500-gallon aquarium installed, I said to Beau: "These fish are my dogs. But unlike dogs, they don't bark, they don't mess up the floor, they don't need me when I'm out of town." Eventually, he came around, says he likes it now. Sometimes even goes over and says "hi" to the fish.

Q: *You said you found this property when you and Beau were out house-hunting. Tell me about the experience.*

Charles: He took me to see space in a high-rise near Bayou Bend. Afterwards, we were driving back to the gallery down Kirby, and all of a sudden he whips into a driveway. If you've ever ridden in a car with Beau, then you know he has two speeds—stop and lightning fast. He's very comfortable behind the wheel, but he doesn't spend a lot of time looking straight ahead. He likes to point out interesting things out the side windows—he never knows what the hell is going on out the front. Kind of frightening to ride with him. If he drank, it would be terrible.

Charles Joekel

ABOVE AND LEFT OVERLEAF: *Quick-Knight residence . . . the clients told Beau they wanted color, and they got it!*

Q: *So, he whips into this driveway—*

Charles: Yes. Beau told me he was building a house for the people who used to live here, and the property was for sale. We looked around and I bought it on the spot.

Q: *Then did you consult with him on renovation, design, furnishings?*

Charles: Let's see. We chose the carpet and I went out of town. When I got back, the house was completely decorated, furnished, and finished. He came swinging in here with his wonderful crew while I was gone and got it done in five days.

Q: *All of his clients and friends are amazed at how fast he works.*

Charles: He has the ability to do things very nicely, and very quickly. One of the reasons is the tremendous inventory in the Brownstone Gallery. Everything Beau's got is for sale. He'd sell you the shoes off his feet for the right price. See those lamps up there? I asked him what kind of lamps they were. He answered, "Oh Charles, they are wonderful! They are solid brass, very old, very old Italian library lanterns." So all of a sudden, I'm getting excited about my lamps. I say, "Are they really?" And Beau smiles and says, "Well, I don't know— they could be."

Q: *Still excited about your lamps?*

Charles: Love them.

Q: *The downstairs guest bathroom is opulent—a throne room fit for a sultan. One of Beau's pet projects is to design fabulous guest bathrooms for his clients.*

Charles: Yes, frankly I've never seen anything like it in my life. Told Beau I christened it "The Royal Flush."

Q: *You and Beau own the wonderful villa in Acapulco together—Las Colinas. How did that business partnership come about?*

Charles: We were staying across the street at Beau's house, Tres Palabras, when Beau said Las Colinas was for sale and we should go over and look at it. Walking up the hill he told me the house was owned by a Mexican general who was in charge of all the Mexican army's operations in South America. Well, perhaps you don't know, but there are no Mexican army operations in South America.

Q: *Beau was teasing you.*

Charles: That's a fair statement.

Q: *But you did do the deal together. You and Beau are both entrepreneurial, with fingers in many pies. Is he a good business partner.*

Charles: There are still people in this world with whom you can shake hands and you don't need anything else. As long as they are alive, they will keep their word. Beau is one of those people. If he tells you he's going to do something, it's my experience that he does it. Scrupulously honest in business deals.

Q: *And apparently rather perceptive when it comes to business speculation.*

Charles: Think about his property in Austin. Not one person in a million would have had the foresight to buy that land on the mountain. My goodness, even if he didn't own the property, consider what he has achieved with The Oasis. It's a Texas landmark. Beau has that touch.

Q: *Can we define that touch?*

Charles: He has the knack to get extraordinary results from ordinary people. People that work for Beau stay with him a long time. I believe it's because he turns them loose, trusts them to do their very best. Take the Brownstone Restaurant. What a success that is—and has been for thirty years. He probably spends less than twenty minutes a week there, but he's got a staff in place that is highly competent. They make it possible for Beau to go on to something else. He does not micromanage.

Q: *It's not a secret that Beau is multitalented. Do you know of any unusual ability— one that's not common knowledge?*

Charles: Yes, he's a geography expert. On the ground and in the air. When flying anywhere between Houston and Mexico, he can look out of the airplane window and tell you where you are. He can even identify the bodies of water down below. So there's another talent—good dead reckoning.

Q: *Do you two plan to partner up on any business ventures in the future?*

Charles: Well, there is the matter of the cars.

Q: *What's the matter with the cars?*

Charles: At present he is vigorously trying to talk me out of my car. I have a 1999 Rolls Royce Silver Sariff, and Beau has a 1974 Cadillac Eldorado convertible that he knows I'm lusting after. So Beau says, "Tell you what I'm going to do, Charles. I'll make you this deal—we'll trade cars for two years, heads up." And I say, "No, no, no! It's not to my benefit economically to do that!" "But you love that Cadillac," he protests. And I keep insisting that a heads up trade is not the best deal for me.

Q: *Who do you think will win in the end?*

Charles: He knows how much I want to buy that wonderful car. Come to think about it, in my opinion he owes me that Cadillac because I did this interview. Of course I might be persuaded to throw in a little cash too.

He has the ability to do things very nicely, and very quickly. One of the reasons is the tremendous inventory in the Brownstone Gallery. Everything Beau's got is for sale. He'd sell you the shoes off his feet for the right price.

—Charles Joekel

Rooms with Viewpoints . . . And Charming Stories

I got my first glimpse of Beau Theriot in 1994 when he went striding through the small Austin store I owned at the time. He walked quickly around, pointing at things and saying: "I want that and that, and that and that." Then, he was gone in a flash.

I thought, who was that fellow with the carriage and the command of a four-star general, commandeering my merchandise by the truckload and leaving without paying for it?

For eight years now, my husband George and I have enjoyed a business relationship and a great friendship with Beau. And I am proud to say, tradition has not been forgotten. Beau still comes into the gallery, picks out this and that and that and this, and leaves without paying for a thing.

—Ann Attal

B eau knows what he likes and what he wants in a matter of minutes. What he doesn't always remember is how many canvases he's bought—he doesn't recall which paintings were selected on previous shopping trips. One picture, for example, has been down in the basement for quite a long time. Once every six months I'll say: "Beau, you like this picture?" He'll get real enthusiastic about the piece and ask me how much it costs. Gives me great pleasure to remind him the picture belongs to him, and has for five years.

—George Attal

Art dealers Ann and George Attal display the works of such masters as Van Gogh, Matisse, and Picasso, as well as paintings by contemporary artists at their internationally prominent Austin Galleries. Beau usually times his shopping trips to the gallery so that he arrives around the noon hour. In the little kitchen behind the art scene, George always has something delicious on the stove. A gourmet chef, the art dealer is as famous for his moussaka as for his Chagalls.

The office of Janine Fertitta with its Bahama mama influence!

Beau, Donna, and Tony Vallone

*B*eau and I have many things in common. We're both perfectionists. We both love what we do, and have made lifelong friendships with many of our clients. We both work long hours and remain consistent in our pledge to do it right or not do it at all. We both love the creative process, and have devoted our lives to it. Don't see either of us ever slowing down. Tell you what, I'll stop when Beau stops. Never is as good a time as any.

—Tony Vallone

*B*eau makes every person he works with feel that their home is the most beautiful he's ever done, and their friendship is the most meaningful.

—Fredell Deutser

Fredell and the kissing bandit

*T*here are still people in this world with whom you can shake hands and you don't need anything else. As long as they are alive, they will keep their word. Beau is one of those people. If he tells you he's going to do something, it's my experience that he does it.

—Charles Joekel

149

ABOVE: *Fredell and Bobby Deutser's entry . . . the collecting never ends*
RIGHT: *Ann and Travis Traylor master bedroom*

All the people he's taken care of for the last twenty-five years still need him in their lives. He decorated our house twenty-five years ago, and except for a few minor adjustments, it has outlasted all the trends. A Beau house is timeless. People need him not just for the decorating; mainly it's for his friendship. The spirit of this amazing man, that's what they're seeking. Beau is like sunshine. I admire how he dials into my taste.

—Karol Barnhart

I grew up in a small house in Ireland where my brothers and I shared one bedroom. You might say I have an intimate knowledge of what the word "cozy" means. When Donna and I began working with Beau, he told us his goal was to achieve a collective look for our new home rather than a furnished look—a jazzy mixture customized to our personal taste as well as being dressed for universal appeal. Grandly beautiful are the grand spaces in our home, yet Beau kept cozy in mind throughout the process.

—Philip Berber

My nickname for Beau is The Tornado. When he comes into The Marketplace (a store adjacent to The Oasis), I grab a notepad and a pen and get ready to take down the "be-sures." He'll have a slew of them: "Be sure to do this, be sure to take care of that." It's all I can do to keep up with him.

—Virginia Ramsey

What Beau did in four hours would have taken another decorator four months.

—Tova and Ace Kindred

ABOVE: *Tova and Ace Kindred love their study.* RIGHT: *The charming library of the Travis Traylors*

A grand staircase in the Traylor residence with custom runner designed by Beau

When he shops, he's like a kid in a toy store—his sister Dianne will back me up on that—but there's a valid explanation. Beau keeps a lot of projects in his mind, and since he has such a good eye for quality, for beauty, for what's unique, when he spots something perfect for one of his clients, he buys it. Buys it immediately.

The notion that when you go out looking for something specific it eludes you, is not a notion Beau fools around with. Wherever he is, whatever shop he's in, in whichever part of the world, Beau knows when he's spotted a must-have. Without a second thought, it's bought, hauled off, set up inside the client's home, and everyone's thrilled to death. And my impetuous friend smiles all the way to the bank.

Working with a creative person like Beau, it rubs off on you. Working with a great talent who's not pretentious, it's nice when that rubs off on you too.

—John Holt

When we first began talking about the design for my house, Beau acknowledged my preference for earth tones—he knows I've never cared much for strong colors.

But he went ahead and brought in the red Oriental and the red Breceda anyway. "That color certainly does wake up the room," I admitted to him. "Red is something I suppose I needed, but just didn't know it."

After the work was finished, to thank him for the exquisite achievement in the design of my home, I presented Beau with a leopard skin hammer, trimmed with marabou. He beamed and said: "Now here's something I've always needed, but— like you Dee—guess I just didn't know it."

—DeAnne Doane

155

$\mathcal{P}$lans for our house were drawn on cocktail napkins, on walls, on lunch sacks. Whenever an idea came to Beau, he'd grab whatever blank surface was in sight and start sketching. Contractor Wayne Beaty would look at the drawing, nod, and the work sailed smoothly onward.

—Kathy Moor

$\mathcal{I}$ called the gallery, introduced myself to Beau over the phone, and told him I had a small room that I wanted decorated. He said "I'll come over," and in five minutes he was there at my front door. I took him into the library, he asked me a few questions, said he would return soon, and was gone in a flash.

Joan and John Bishop with Beau

A few hours later, he was back with a truck and a few men. By 4:00 P.M. the library was transformed, magnificently designed with furniture, accessories, paintings—finished and perfect. I invited him to come back around six to meet my husband John.

At the appointed time, Beau arrived. As John and I were expressing our admiration for the library, we looked across into the living room and saw Beau placing two objects on the mantel above the fireplace. John says—John's from Waco—John says, "Beau, I see sumthin' in the livin' room. We did not give you the livin' room, boy!" Beau says, "Let me tell you what I think needs to happen in the living room."

And he does tell us, in detail. About halfway through, John stops Beau and says, "Okay, how much for the whole damn house, boy?" And that was that. We were happily hooked. What Beau offers is instantaneous success. The motto of his business is "now," no waiting necessary. He is a trinity of talent, energy, and inventory.

—Joan Bishop

The Quick-Knights' colorful living room

156

I LIVE ON GOOD SOUP, NOT ON

The Quick-Knight kitchen shows Beau is "a little bit country!"

Beau never gets upset when something is broken. His theory is, whatever you have should be used. Break it, and that just verifies the fact that the object played an active part in the home. He also doesn't mind if something is chipped or marred. Beau says that's part of the character—part of the life of the object. Beauty doesn't have to be perfect to be beautiful. He's taught me how to look at things differently.

We've traveled together quite a lot. And no matter where we've been—walking down the street in Manhattan, strolling through the French Quarter in New Orleans—invariably people will come up and say: "Well, hi Beau!" Everywhere we go, somebody knows Beau. The charming thing about it is, he knows every one of them too. Never met a man with so many friends.

—George Pelletier

George Pelletier with Beau and Señor

Great hall in the Pelletier Dallas residence

With the indisputable authority of a four-star general, Beau can be quick, decisive, and not easily bucked. I remember the day he sold me my office furniture. He had come to my office to discuss a legal matter, not my interior décor. But he took one look around, said "Okay, I'll be back," and was out the door. A few hours

later, a truck pulled up, and men began unloading stuff. Beau came in and placed the new furniture around the room. Then he said "You need a painting." He was off again. Thirty minutes later he was back with a picture of hunting dogs. He hammered in a nail and hung the painting.

All I can say is, it's very pleasurable to be around someone who knows exactly what he's doing and can convince me I know what I'm doing at the same time.

—Tom Bousquet

I met his talent first. Then I moved heaven and earth (and Mexico) to meet Beau in person. My husband and I looked at a house for sale in River Oaks that Beau had decorated for the builder. We decided we wanted the house, along with every stick of furniture, every design element, everything down to the smallest flower vase.

So I called the Brownstone Gallery, and told them to add it up. The person on the phone said I would have to speak to Beau Theriot to get accurate pricing, but he was away, vacationing at his house in Acapulco. I asked for the number and called him. When he answered, I asked, "What are you doing down there when I need you up here?" Beau paused a minute, explained that he was on vacation, and as an afterthought asked, "Who is this?"

I said: "This is Mary Laminack. I just bought that house over on Inverness. Would you please get home, we've got some work to do." He came home immediately.

At our first meeting, he gave me the bottom line. I remember saying, "No, no, no," and then I think I repeated myself. I told him to take it all back to the gallery—to back a truck up to the front door and haul it away. Then I reconsidered, decided to split the difference. Told him to take half of it away.

As the Army was loading up the stuff that would be returned to the gallery, he uttered the famous Beau line—the line that every client he's ever worked with has heard once, some maybe three or four times. "Mary," he said, "you're swallowing camels and choking on gnats." That was Beau's way of saying, "Mary, you've got a great house—a great house needs great stuff." I must admit, it was a very sheepish client that called him a few days later to ask if she could please have the other half of the great stuff brought back.

We've been friends for many years. When I asked Beau to decorate the ranch in Wimberly, we butted heads as usual during the process. In the end, he had his way, as usual. You know what ticks me off? In every suggestion, in every vision, he's always right!

—Mary Laminack

Beau and Mary Laminack

B̶eau's gift is not something you could box and tie up with a ribbon. If you could, it would be better than anything ever offered in Neiman's Christmas catalog.

—Shirley Shaw

RIGHT OVERLEAF: *Quick-Knight family room with colors built around their art over the fireplace*

Elise and Uncle Beau

As a little girl, I used to spend time with Uncle Beau at his first lake house in Austin. One of my best memories is of the quiet man—the Beau of reflection. We would lounge together and gaze out at the lake through two big windows for hours. When the sun went down, he would read and I would watch television. Just being together meant a lot to both of us. All of my life, he's been like a father to me; we have a special bond. He took me under his wing. About those wings—there has always been room under them for any member of the family who needed help or encouragement.

—Elise Kamins

From my earliest memories of Beau, from junior high school through high school, college, and on into life, I remember most his eternal optimism, love of life and beauty, concern for others, and lighthearted banter. Growing up in a small blue-collar town, we enjoyed a simple youth with strong parental guidance, but not so strong that we didn't do our share of pranks. One of our favorites was to frustrate the "little old plant ladies" in the neighborhood by taking pot plants late at night from one porch and exchanging them for plants from the next-door neighbor, leading, we believed, to interesting confrontations the following morning. We also traveled together on our first big adventures—camping in Colorado in high school and exploring New York City early in our college years, Beau's outgoing knowing-no-stranger way compensating for my much more reserved nature.

—Dan F. Smith

Beau makes magic. When you're with him, the days and nights are magical. He's the Wizard of Ahs. The world would be a lot better if there were more people like Nadine Theriot. Beau didn't have a chance to be selfish, dumb, or a failure—he's his mother's son.

—Joan Brown

If I had to name one thing that Beau will never be any good at, it's fishing. To fish means to sit and wait—that would drive Beau crazy. So I go alone. For many years I used a very primitive method. My only gear was a string and a hook. I'd tie the string to my finger, then hope the fish wouldn't be too big or it might pull me in. I never keep the fish I catch, but always throw them back. The fun is in the experience, something only a fisherman would understand.

Once when I returned to the house after a couple hours spent down at the lake— and returned with no fish as usual—Beau

J. T. Trevino and friend . . . a fish tale

suggested I take up another sport because what kind of fisherman always comes home with no fish. So, the next day I took my string and my hook to the lake, caught ten fish in thirty minutes, wrapped them in my shirt, and took them home. In triumph, I presented Beau with the contents of my very stinky shirt. He went straight out and bought me a fishing pole, a basket for carrying the catch, and a new shirt.

—Juan de Dios (J. T.) Trevino

Joan Brown and Shirley Raines with Beau

Beau likes it when his companions are just as adventurous as he is. And when he's out on the hunt—shopping trips—he admires those who will stay with him, who never get tired. If you are a pal who will stay with the shopping safari from the moment the stores open until closing time—no matter how much your feet hurt—he reckons you an accomplished big game hunter.

—Shirley Raines

165

I've traveled the highways, the byways, the dirt roads, and the hairpin curves of the world with Beau. We've been vagabonds through the backwaters and typical tourists through the glittering cities; we've strolled the boulevards, climbed the mountains, and made our way barefoot to the beaches together. I remember one car trip that brought us down from the Canadian interior into the United States. Exhaustion demanded we stop to sleep, but it was well past midnight before we finally spotted the only "Vacancy" sign between Quebec and southernmost Maine. Beau likes stumbling across out-of-the-way places—places where the motel sign is missing a few bulbs, where the tourist cabins have seen better days, where there's only a bug light to see by, even inside the cabin. It's his insatiable sense of adventure that draws him to such spots. I admit I slept with one eye open on that particular night. Beau slept like a baby.

—James Johnston

James Johnston, right, with Beau and J. T.

*B*eau with his long legs, me with these short legs, everywhere we've ever gone together, I have to run to keep up with him. He's always on a mission, can't sit still for two minutes. And he's always thinking, thinking as fast as he moves. A great deal of that thinking is about other people's pleasure, other people's comfort. For example, when he decorated our high-rise residence, he kept in mind our active young grandchildren and rounded the corners on all the tables.

—Barbara La Grange

When I first met Beau's father, even though in his senior years at the time, I was impressed by the striking similarity between father and son. Both men of stature, strong and handsome, personable. Later, Beau told me an interesting story—a memory from when he was a young man working at his dad's lumberyard.

Beau said, "I remember studying my father's hands. He worked with his hands every day—they were big, masculine hands, hands of strength, hands capable of doing the most difficult work. Then I looked down at my own hands. They were different. They looked almost delicate, and I wondered, can I ever live up to my father? Can I ever expect to have his strength, fill those hands?"

Well, of course, we are all witnesses to Beau's strength and his capacity for hard work. I think any credible palm reader could have explained the life line to the young man. Beau was seeing the future in the hands of an artist."

Patricia Kepke and Q-Tip

—Patricia Kepke

Marc and Melissa Deer

My husband and I had not had good experiences with decorators—we referred to them as the "D-word." When I told Marc there was a designer I would like him to meet, he frowned and growled a protest. Then Marc met Beau. There have been no more fights about the "D-word" in our house. . . . I want to be one of those women who say, "I've known Beau for thirty years, and this is the sixth house he's done for me."

—Melissa Deer

167

Mexico
Seasoning of
All Enjoyments

SEÑOR BEAU

The flight from Houston to Acapulco was an easy two hours. Enough time for a Bloody Mary, a couple of chapters of Spanish vocabulary, and a nap. Scattered around in seats throughout the save-the-money-for-the-jewelry Economy Class section were longtime friends, business associates, and a few new friends who were on their first adventure to Mexico with Señor Beau. The final destination would be Casa Las Colinas, one of the three homes Beau owns in Acapulco, along with Casa Tres Palabras and Villa Carey. Any one of these gorgeous examples of exterior and interior design could pose for the centerfold of *Architectural Digest*.

It is a wonderful seasoning of all enjoyments to think of those we love.

—Molière

As is the custom when traveling with Beau, an entourage was on board. The party would leave the muddy Gulf behind and fly west through a bunch of bouncy billowy clouds, landing at last at the edge of the blue Pacific. If the assembled group of ten appeared as eager as scouts following along after a camp counselor, the explanation is simple: Beau likes people. And he likes a whole lot of people to be on hand when he hosts a convivial journey into the well-loved land south of the border.

The travelers, mostly unknown to each other, shared a common exuberance. For whether an intimate or new to the fold, everyone understood that when in the company of Beau, the company is king. Beau hosts company very nicely indeed. One senses it is his greatest pleasure. He had chosen his travel ensemble—both in the choice of his companions and in selection of his wardrobe—to reflect a theme of eclecticism.

About the outfit. No one would ever accuse Beau of being a clotheshorse. Instead, he is a Thoreau-back. Just as the author of *Walden* advised against fussy peacockery when choosing coverings for the body, Beau prefers dressing for comfort, no matter what the occasion. When in Acapulco, he opts for the ever-varied hues of an Hawaiian shirt, black Bermuda shorts, sockless loafers. Maybe a baseball cap if he spends extended time in the sun. He carried a couple of quickly packed carry-on bags. His closet in the master suite at his primary home, Casa Tres Palabras, was amply stocked with shirts, shorts, shoes, and bathing suits left behind on previous trips.

*Beau appreciates the extraordinary craftsmanship of the Mexican people,
their work ethic, and their ability to see beyond the conventional
to new ideas in construction, in artwork, in design.*

$\mathcal{B}$eau Theriot, who owns the Brownstone Restaurant and is one of Houston's
top interior designers, celebrated his big 5-0 birthday during the Labor Day weekend
at his Acapulco retreat, Casa Tres Palabras. The "season" south of the border may
have been technically over, but you couldn't have told it from Beau's 50 guests or
the festivities that constantly popped up over the long weekend...Beau hosted special
dinners from Wednesday night through the big birthday dinner on Saturday night.
A few of those on hand roasting and toasting the birthday boy were his mom, Nadine
Theriot; his sister, Dianne Maspero, and Dianne's daughter, Elise Braden.
Guests came from Mexico City, Argentina, Tennessee, New York, Mississippi
and all around Texas. Among the Houston group were Frann Lichtenstein,
Fredell and Bobby Deutser, Julian and Janeen Fertitta, Dr. John and Joan Bishop,
and Linda Knight and hubby Mark Quick.

—Maxine Mesinger,
"Big City Beat," *Houston Chronical*, September 9, 1996

172

Knowing that I was going through a bad time in my life, Beau asked, "What are you doing Labor Day? Want to come to my birthday party?" I thanked him and said I certainly would like to attend. "By the way," he added, "the party's in Acapulco!" After just 24 hours spent among his friends in Acapulco, I went back to my room and wrote down the names of 32 people I had met—32 warm and gracious people. Some wonderful, life-changing experiences on that trip. Beau offers a gift better than gold—he shares his friends with friends.

—Maud Ella Hartley

Even when he's dressed down, people tend to look up to him. With a forward gaze that rarely varies, and dark features—eyes, hair, complexion—asserting his Spanish-French lineage, he could be a prince making a journey incognito. An unarmored Sir Lancelot headed for a tropical vacation disguised in beachcomber clothes.

Those traveling with him were a duke's mixture of personalities as different as chalk from cheese. Delighted to see his dinner table circled with a variety of characters, Beau appreciates the concept of striking sparks, maybe even igniting fireworks in the intimate bosom of company. Happy whenever there's a lively exchange, he leans in with great expectation when a guest begins to come to life verbally. He also derives pleasure from telling anecdotes from his own experience, so conversation at Beau's round table invariably escalates into a bonanza of fine storytelling. Interaction never lags, mainly because people feel at ease, sensing their host would be the first to get the joke, first to listen and understand, the last to censor.

Beau enjoys setting the conversational circle with dissimilar personalities to create a very singular, very vibrant social canvas for chat, for singing, for dancing, for recitation, even for stand-up comedy. To see someone suddenly put down the breakfast fork, pull an original poem from the bodice of a bathing suit, and begin to recite during the morning huevos rancheros is not an uncommon occurrence.

And just as suddenly, there is the pleasure of finding a new friend. Like the ripple effect, Beau's personal friends become personal friends among themselves. It is his most gracious ulterior motive.

Havens On The Hill

Tiered down a hill in the lovely Balcones de la Luna area, Beau's three magnificent villa retreats overlook Acapulco Bay, and each is fashioned with his signature style. Casa Tres Palabras, the name of the middle structure, which was his first purchase in Acapulco, translates as "the house of three words." The three words could be nothing else but "I love you."

Outstanding among the generally outstanding villas in the neighborhood, Tres Palabras comfortably sleeps up to fourteen people, and should a dinner party be on the agenda, a couple more guests may be invited, as armchairs around the dining tables number sixteen. Should the mood strike to throw a party for one hundred nearest and dearest, there are three large entertainment areas, an oversized swimming pool, an innovative sunning area where lounge chairs are set directly in an ankle-high wading pool, and a kitchen wherein the genius of resident chef Magdalena is always at work.

Just down the hill, the bone-white, Mediterranean-style, four-story Villa Carey is a singularly glorious structure. As with the other two homes, there is an unobstructed view of the city across the waters of the vibrantly blue bay. Beau conceived and designed Villa Carey, and built it in partnership with his friend Laura Cuevas, with construction executed by builder Javier Larios. Their collaboration achieved a superlative retreat in Mexico's favorite resort town. It is leased to a local businessman who occupies the villa as residence, and it is not currently utilized as a place to entertain guests. However, Villa Carey is on the market.

173

The open-air great room at Las Colinas, one of the "fiesta-friendly" casas where the travelers from Texas spent the week with Señor Beau

Ode To Beau

Beau, Beau, the genius man.
He can decorate like nobody can.

Tell him your colors, tell him your style,
He'll create a dream house in a little while.

He'll take you shopping, he'll take you bopping,
He'll keep you hopping in Acapulco.

He's so decisive, says, "This is it."
With another designer it wouldn't fit.

We love him and he loves us.
He loves to make a fuss over us.

He's a big man with a great big heart,
Kind, strong, handsome, funny, and smart.

The host with the most and a staff so dear,
Let's all stand up and give a big cheer for...

Beau, Beau, the genius man.
He can decorate like nobody can!

—Performed by friends at Beau's birthday party

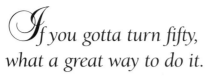

*If you gotta turn fifty,
what a great way to do it.*

176

Located just up the hill from Tres Palabras, surrounded by fire engine–red adobe walls and accessed through massive double wrought-iron gates, stands the home that must be described as fiesta-friendly—Casa Las Colinas. It is here that the travelers from Texas will spend a week with Beau. Like Tres Palabras, Las Colinas is an open-air wonder. Walking down a winding stone path nestled between huge pots of flourishing hot pink bougainvillea, and entering the beautifully furnished sala (the grand main living room of the house), a person unfamiliar with Mexico's fair weather might blurt out: "Where are the walls!"

"We left them back in Houston," says Beau, leading the way past another puzzle. Settled in for the duration, firmly planted on its haunches in the wall-less main room is a giant rock. It's a massive granite monolith that rolled down the hill during the glacial period and has remained adamantly ensconced for a millennium. Respectful of the rock's venerable tenure, Beau invited it to take up permanent residence inside his house in the hills.

Under The Mayan Palapa

At Las Colinas, the keeper of the kitchen is a talented genial woman named Modesta. Down the hill at Beau's larger home, Tres Palabras, with the kitchen under the command of the thirty-five-year culinary career soldier, Magdalena, there is little reason to leave the compound to go in search of delicious food. In these two houses exists the best cooking in Acapulco.

Both women are experts in the preparation of ceviche—a dish of Peruvian origin in which raw fish "cooks" in lime juice, then is mixed with tomatoes and onions and other ingredients particular to the style of the creator. Magdalena's version of ceviche is a veritable fish potpourri.

Colorful and always surprising, scenically lovely, made lovelier still by the charm of its people, Mexico is an elixir to Beau—a revitalizing tonic, his fountain of youth.

—James Johnston

Modesta's version of ceviche combines mango and papaya with onion and tomato and is limited to shrimp only. No other fish goes into the mix. Sharing equal billing as stars of the mashed avocado, both chefs do something with guacamole that must be the envy of every Mexican food restaurant in Heaven.

It is a tradition at both Tres Palabras and Las Colinas to offer guests a communal bowl of guacamole and individual servings of ceviche immediately upon arrival. Any fussy protesting about unpacking and hanging up clothes so they won't wrinkle may be a victory for unwrinkled clothes, but the neatnik will miss out on the guacamole. Usually the last chip hits the bottom of the guacamole bowl in two minutes flat.

This tasteful welcome is offered at Las Colinas in the open-air circle of comfortable couches and chairs that are set under the Mayan palapa. Juxtaposed to the swimming pool, the Mayan palapa gazes directly across the pool at the Aztec palapa. A jungle of color in Beau's perfectly maintained private garden surrounds both palapas. Guests enjoy soft breezes blowing through verdant tropicals, mango trees with lavalieres of plump fruit, a cluster of outlandishly constructed red flowers that are impossible to identify, the varying hues of bougainvillea that grow here as lush and as insistent as the bluebonnet fields in Texas.

A palapa is a gazebo, south-of-the-border style. The difference in construction derives from the methods employed.

An inviting table at Casa Tres Palabras

Modesta's Muy Delicioso Salad Dressing

Makes 1 cup

2 heaping tablespoons sugar
2 heaping tablespoons large capers
1 heaping tablespoon black pepper
2 large garlic cloves
1 heaping tablespoon salt
1/2 cup extra-virgin olive oil
1/4 cup apple cider vinegar

Combine the sugar, capers, pepper, garlic
and salt in a blender. Add the olive oil and
vinegar and process until smooth.

The luncheon table passes Juan's inspection.

An excellent majordomo, Juan is the quintessential example of a Beau employee: capable, smart, aware of all that is going on around him, cordial, industrious, loyal, and ready to express opinion when he feels strongly about something. For example, green beans.

After a few remarks are exchanged about the seasonal freshness of items to be purchased at the local market, Juan hands Beau a spiral notebook and a pen. Modesta's famous key lime pie is the first order of business. Juiced with four limes of the tiny, sour variety, it reigns as triumph of the house. Writing "key lime pie" across the top of the page, Beau adds an emphatic exclamation point.

Dessert decided, the colloquy between the two men turns to the subject of sea bass. Juan asks if Señor Beau would like green beans served with the lightly battered, sautéed sea bass. Mashed potatoes having already been agreed upon, the debate looms regarding green beans versus squash. Beau opts for squash—calabasita. Juan continues to quietly promote the freshness of the market's green beans.

In rapid-fire order the menu fills up with breakfast, lunch, and dinner items planned for the next seven days. Saying that he guessed he would go ahead and pick up a sack of green beans anyway while at the market—"just in case,"—Juan leaves the house to go shopping.

Ancient cultures first created the individualistic thatched palapa structures. Both palapas have thatched roofs made of weathered, gray-brown palm leaves that overlap and overhang the basic configuration. The Aztec variety has a roof design that resembles the symmetry of a parasol—a parasol with a nipple on top. The Mayan palapa is more involved. Looked at straight on, the primary roof is angled at 90 degrees, at both the west and east ends; then it vaults up at the center and goes flat, giving the palapa the appearance of having visited a barber to get a crew cut. Above the Mayan palapa, a soaring mango tree thick with fruit adorns the crew cut with a jaunty headdress.

While guests try to avoid getting into fist fights over guacamole dipping, Beau confers with Juan, the house manager, about the week's menus.

To thank Beau for inviting me to his house in Acapulco, I presented him with a silk shirt that was beautifully made, really fine, an alternative to the Hawaiian shirts he so adores. He put it on, then promptly spilled guacamole down the front. "Esther," he said, with those black eyes twinkling humorously, "you know I love the shirt, but it needed the official initiation—every shirt I own has a guacamole stain on it!" I remember Beau wore my gift the next day too, stain proudly visible.

—Esther Smith

Rosca Japonaisa (Japanese Rose)

Serves 8 to10

Custard
3 (15-ounce) cans evaporated milk
1 cup sour cream
3 large spoons sugar
5 envelopes unflavored gelatin
1 cup cold water

Rose Topping
1 pint frozen strawberries
1 large spoon sugar

For the custard, combine the evaporated milk, sour cream and sugar in a large saucepan and bring to a boil. Cook until the sugar dissolves, stirring constantly. Reduce the heat to medium-low and keep the mixture hot. Soften the gelatin in the cold water in a double boiler or a small saucepan. Place over boiling water and cook until the gelatin dissolves completely.

Stir the gelatin into the hot evaporated milk mixture. Pour into a bowl and place the bowl in cold water. Let stand until cool. Pour the cooled mixture into a flan pan with a tube center. Chill until firm. Invert onto a large plate.

For the topping, combine the strawberries and sugar in a blender just before serving and process until smooth; pour into the center hole of the flan. Drizzle lines across the flan.

Las Colinas Key Lime Pie

Serves 8

1 (14-ounce) can sweetened condensed milk
2 (15-ounce) cans evaporated milk
8 ounces cream cheese, softened
juice of 6 Key limes
1 package Gamesa-Marias cookies
    (available at Fiesta stores and
    specialty markets) or vanilla wafers
butter

Combine the condensed milk, evaporated milk, cream cheese and lime juice in a blender and process until smooth and creamy; process in 2 batches if necessary.

Arrange a layer of the cookies in a buttered 9×13-inch dish and spoon 1/3 of the lime mixture over the cookies. Repeat the layers twice, using all the ingredients. Cover with waxed paper and freeze for 4 hours or longer. Thaw before slicing to serve.

Modesta's famous Key Lime Pie, Las Colinas

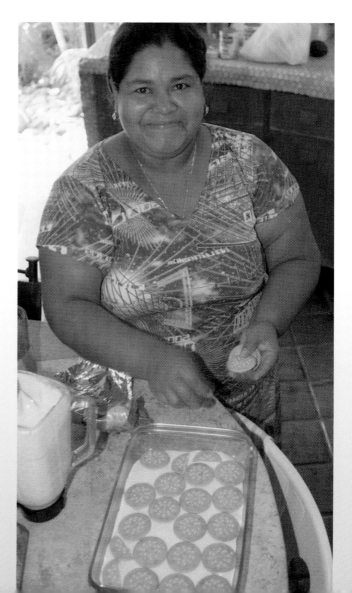

*So every night I prayed in bed (and threw in a few novenas),
please, dear Lord, when I am dead, make my reward Las Colinas!*

Noting customary hours for dining in Mexico, Beau advises his guests that the coffeepot will be out at 7 A.M. for early risers. Breakfast at 10, lunch at 2:30, teatime (make that guacamole time) at 4, dinner at 9:30, dessert served under the Mayan palapa around 10:30.

Any worry about waistline expansion is cut short by the arrival of the Massage Brigade. Neatly outfitted in navy blue shorts, white cotton shirts and tennis shoes, a contingent of six therapists, none over the age of 25, parades into the palapa, announcing their readiness to go to work. Unfolding tables, assembling creams and oils, the Massage Brigade sets up shop under the Mayan palapa.

Three of Beau's male guests decide to partake of the brigade's services. As the next order of business, it is suggested the three males strip down to their underdrawers. Upon discovering that the cover-ups provided to preserve modesty were no bigger than cup towels—for both gentlemen and ladies—several female guests politely tiptoe away. Beau laughs and says: "It takes awhile to get acclimated to Paradise."

Dealing In The Sand

Beau does not mix different design styles or cultures in Acapulco. Loving Mexico as he does and admiring its artisans, he sticks strictly with the region when decorating. Repeated visits over the years to the markets in Quadalajara, in Mexico City, and in the more remote areas of the country qualify him as a connoisseur of Mexican artistry. As a collector of the form, Beau's eye for what is beautiful, for what is unusual, for the wonderful never misses. The three homes lend testimony.

That he keeps a discriminating eye ever vigilant and on the lookout for treasure has been demonstrated within these pages. It should also be noted that Beau loves to ace a great deal. A particular purchase, made in an unusual setting, is a story worth repeating.

One afternoon, after the guests had enjoyed several days luxuriating at Las Colinas, Beau announced that it was time to make a trip to a spot down the coastline that he calls "the primitive beach." Even though the thought of a "primitive beach" might conjure visions of wild men frolicking bare-bottomed through shark-infested waters, some of the more adventurous hopped in the van, ready to face any peril as long as Beau was guide. Van packed with swimming suit–clad worthies, Beau took the wheel.

Thirty minutes up the road, he turned off the main highway and headed down a narrow two-lane strip toward the beach. That this was an area plagued by poverty was readily discerned. Shacks set among burned-out palm fields defined the nature of the neighborhood. It was apparent to all on board that the glamour of tourist-loving Acapulco had been left far behind.

Photographer James Innes enjoying therapy under the Mayan palapa at Las Colinas

Always refreshing, always blooming, the pool at Tres Palabras

Casa Tres Palabras' palapa is the ultimate Mexican setting for the camaraderie guests enjoy.

A Better Place

With open arms I welcome you,
Please come in and share my space—
Your smile and personality
Will make this a better place.

With open arms I beckon you,
Please open up your heart—
Express your deepest feelings
And make all of us a part.

So many empty pleasures
Would be mine without you near—
I just want to hug you
And say how glad I am you're here.

Yes, my dear, I cherish you,
And the friendship I see upon your face—
Without you, I would perish—true!
You make this a better place.

—Beau

LEFT: Beau's collection of pre-Columbian-style stone figures by Mexican artisans graces the gardens at Beau's homes in Acapulco.

Seemingly separated from the creature comforts of Las Colinas not only by miles, but by centuries, the van penetrated into the wild, undeveloped environs of the Mexican outback. To the right, flanking the small backwater rusticity of a village called Barra Viejo, a march of crudely constructed beach bars appeared to be the only viable local commerce. Bar proprietors had sent forth young, barefoot barkers to stand at roadside hawking the attractions of their dilapidated watering sheds. These native publicists promoted with aggressive enthusiasm—waving in the odd bus or van that they hoped carried passels of thirsty people. Inside the unprepossessing stick structures, proprietors hoped to soon put their bottle openers to use. They dreamed of being overrun with tourists willing to part with pesos for rounds of beer, lime-topped and not very cold. Here, as is standard everywhere in the world where dollars are needed, the customer is king, the lady with the purse is queen.

Beau turned the van into the parking lot of one of these establishments, mentioning that this particular bar was not his favorite. He had opted to bypass his usual spot because it appeared crowded with a bus tour of sightseers from Germany. Wisely, Beau suspected the German affection for beer would soon deplete the favorite bar's limited supply. Several of the friends on board the van had visited the primitive beach during prior trips to Mexico with Beau. Trial and error had taught these friends not to fall prey to the $45.00 pony rides. Nor would these veterans venture into the sea. Nor would they eat food brought from the rustic kitchens that dotted the primitive beach.

Beau would. As a matter-of-fact, he has great appetite for the grilled whole redfish served at the favorite bar presently crammed with beer-guzzling Germans. Singing the praises of the chef who prepares the delectable redfish—a woman of cheery spirit and nimbleness in the culinary

Shirley Raines inspecting jewelry at the primitive beach

arts practiced over an open-air cook pot—Beau expressed disappointment that his friends would not have the opportunity to meet her.

One of the veterans of the journey to the primitive beach noted that Beau's generosity to the redfish cooker's children has been an ongoing tradition. For that matter, all of the children in the vicinity—children who use the beach as a place of work rather than play—have experienced the beneficence of Señor Beau.

And this was definitely a working beach. Beau's guests, inundated by peddlers offering wares best described as nonessentials, inspected strung beads, key rings, bracelets that begged the age-old question of to be silver or not to be silver, woven trinkets that seemed devoid of meaningful utility, and pictures of impermanent tattoos. More than anything else, the tattoos caught the imagination of the crowd. Beach peddlers offered a book displaying various designs that could be water-washed on the body. Many of the ladies in the company chose to have butterfly imprints teasingly imprinted near cleavage. The men asked for lightning streaks to be emblazoned across the muscle on their shoulders.

Kidding around at Barra Viejo

While his friends were being impermanently inked, Beau settled into a hammock to relax, to enjoy sounds of his friends' laughter, to enjoy the breezes, to enjoy some highly uncommon moments in his life—moments when he was required to do absolutely nothing at all.

And then came the mask man. When the youthful, shirtless, barefoot beach peddler approached, Beau seemed to be fast asleep. Curiously, the young Mexican boy chose not take his wares to the group, but instead sidled up to Beau. If he intended to interrupt Beau's siesta, it was a fair assumption that the peddler and the treasure hunter had had dealings in the past.

The boy drew a ceramic mask from a pouch that was slung around his bare shoulders. It was glazed with a dark blue color as fine as the finest lapis lazuli. The object was unique and surprisingly beautiful, with the contours associated with one of the ancient Aztec gods. The boy did not utter a word, but stood patiently waiting. Hat covering his eyes, not moving a muscle, Beau suddenly spoke. "Cuánto cuestan?" he asked, requesting the price.

The boy wanted twenty dollars American. Beau removed his hat and sat up. Having decided at first glance from beneath his baseball cap that the mask was a worthy treasure, Beau got ready to haggle.

188

Both negotiators fully expected to play the haggling game. Bargaining is a ritual of old tradition, and whether in a fancy shop in downtown Acapulco or vocalized above the sound of the sea at the primitive beach, quibbling over price is the salsa that adds flavor to the deal. When they had finished volleying figures, the sand settled and Beau handed over twelve dollars.

Thanking the young Mexican kindly, Beau received his prize, showered the young boy with candy, and then the two of them—the man who loves beauty and the peddler with unexpected beauty to sell—spent the rest of the afternoon chatting in Spanish about everything under the sun.

Partnership In Design

Laura Cuevas is a friend and business partner who grew up acclimated to this particular paradise. A woman of spirited vivacity, Laura has been an interior decorator, furniture maker and gallery owner in Mexico City for thirty years. Crediting Beau as her mentor, Laura says everything she knows about interior design was learned studying with the master. As both Beau and Laura have been entrepreneurial in their lives, their shared interest in real estate speculation eventually led to partner ownership of Villa Carey.

In 1999, Laura was selected to be a member of an elite group of talents employed to renovate Mexico City's legendary Chapultepec palace, a three-year project completed in 2001. Laura assumed responsibility for upholstery and trimmings, restoration of furniture, curtains to cover 236 windows, and in her own words: "I did all the beds."

The story of her quarter-century friendship with Beau began in Houston—and it began with love at first sight.

The mask man at the beach

RIGHT OVERLEAF: View of Acapulco from the pool at Villa Carey

189

THE LEGS OF ATLAS

A Remembrance by Laura Cuevas

Beau and Laura Cuevas

. . . perfection whispers inside his head.

In the late 1970s, I was hired to decorate a home in Mexico City in the classic French style and decided to make a shopping trip to Houston to search for items appropriate to the project. Just by chance, I wandered into the Brownstone Gallery.

Immediately realizing that the gigantic space was filled with exquisite objects—pieces that were perfectly suited to the desires of my clients back home—I began the selection process, asking for this and that and that and that to be tagged for purchase. The selection soon tallied a considerable amount of money—more than $50,000. I asked to see the gallery owner and was introduced to Beau's sister, Dianne, who asked if she could be of assistance since the owner was not presently in the store.

Smiling, I got straight to the point: "I want a better price." I saw that my request had shocked her, so I gently explained: "We Mexicans are used to bargaining, you see." At that exact moment, the door opened, and in walked a young man so handsome I was certain he had to be a movie star. Dressed in blue jeans and a mink jacket trimmed in leather, he had the sort of presence to wear mink and get away with it. Very slim, with a mustache that made him look like a bandido, and what woman can resist an aspect of danger in a man. I saw his beautiful face and fell in love on the spot.

When Dianne offered to introduce me, I responded, "No, no, no! I want to speak to the owner, not the son of the owner!" Dianne started laughing, took my hand, led me over to the Adonis, and said: "Beau, we have here a client who wants to haggle with you."

Amazed is the natural state when you hang around a lot with Beau.

Star-struck, all I could say was: "Hello, I am a Mexican." Beau smiled. "I love Mexico and Mexicans with a passion," he said. "Shall we sit down and do some horse trading?"

Our friendship began at that moment. By the end of the day, I had invited Beau to visit me in Mexico. "Bring your family," I told him, "and I will welcome you to my vacation home, Valle de Bravo, that overlooks a beautiful lake." Very soon after, Beau flew to Mexico City and I was there to meet him at the airport. Beau walked through the gate with an entourage. Accompanying him were many family members and a few of his assistants. Beau always travels with a big group. The first thing they said to me was, "Don't worry, we can sleep four to a room." That broke the ice, and I fell in love with his family as quickly as I'd fallen for him.

At the end of our first vacation together, my admiration for Beau's mother Nadine was tantamount to worship—she is an exceptional woman. I said to myself, "If I should marry one day, to be successful I must imitate Nadine." I am convinced that Beau received his appreciation for beauty from his mother. Their styles are different, of course—Beau is very *Architectural Digest* and Nadine is *Colonial Homes*, but the common ground is perfection. Perfection guides their handiwork, perfection whispers inside their heads.

I began traveling to Houston often to see Beau, and to learn from him. He became my master, my mentor. Very generously, he took me with him on decorating jobs and patiently explained each step, every aspect of design—how he makes decisions, how to envision a room.

He spoke of the necessity of keeping to schedule, working beyond the call of duty, what it means to be passionately inspired. "Laurita," he said to me, "to win the interest of sophisticated clientele, you must fascinate them with sophisticated planning."

His love of Mexico and the Mexican people delighted me. Beau has in his employ more than one hundred Mexicans. They are his friends and, on occasion, a source of his inspiration. He appreciates the extraordinary craftsmanship of the Mexican people, their work ethic, and their ability to see beyond the conventional to new ideas in construction, in artwork, in design. After making many trips during which he gave close scrutiny to mountain construction in Acapulco, he said, "They build these wonderful, complicated structures on the sides of hills—massive and intricate. Americans are just too timid to try what appears to be the impossible."

When, at last, the stars were perfectly aligned, signaling the time was right for us to collaborate on a project together, Beau and I built Villa Carey down the hill from his house Tres Palabras in Acapulco. As others have observed when relating stories of how Beau begins a construction project, he sketched the plans for the house on a cocktail napkin to begin the vision for Villa Carey. Then he sketched dining room, living room, bedrooms, everything on a succession of cocktail napkins. These instructions were turned over to our architect, and building began. I was amazed. But amazed is the natural state when you hang around a lot with Beau.

The final thing I have to say concerns his legs. Everyone has seen that man who is holding up the world in front of Rockefeller Center in New York City. What's his name? Atlas? Well, Atlas and Beau have the same beautiful legs. It makes me very happy that these days Beau chooses to dress predominantly in Bermuda shorts.

194

Villa Carey presents the glamourous allure of Acapulco's exciting lifestyle.

Feliz Viaje

Another friend, James Johnston, discovered the paradise that is Mexico through his travels with Beau. The acquaintance, however, began in the world of finance. James Johnston met Beau for the first time in Austin in the mid-1970s. They greeted each other along orthodox lines—straightforward eye contact and a cordial handshake. Then Beau asked if could borrow some money. "He presented himself as a man of great poise and assurance," James recalls, "so I saw no reason not to give him what he asked for."

It should perhaps be noted here that the man with the Dickenslike ability to tell a colorful and detailed story toiled in the money field before retiring from banking in 1987. At the time of their initial business encounter, Beau wanted to purchase a house on the lake in Austin and had come to the bank to seek local financing. The banker and the fledgling entrepreneur became instant pals.

Their friendship, which has lasted more than a quarter of a century, transcended the subdued confines of the institution of finance and came to full blossom in the freewheeling, breezy air of shared experience. Simpatico from the beginning, James admires Beau because "he always does what he says he will do," and Beau continues to be intrigued by the fount of knowledge inside the brain of his erudite friend.

They share a mutual love for traveling, going off to see the world at the drop of a hat. In twenty-five years, lots of hats have been dropped, but, recollecting a hard rule of their trips together, James says, "In all of my travels with Beau, we've never had a hotel reservation!

"It should be pointed out that on our driving excursions Beau prefers to take sole command of the wheel, with a sense of direction that is rather uncanny. Not once in our travels across Canada, North America, Europe, or Mexico have I seen him consult a map. He just seems to know which way to go. I have a suspicion he studies the routes secretly, when nobody's looking.

"My assigned duty, during these long drives, is to talk. Talk about everything under the sun. Beau is interested in so many subjects, his inquiring mind likes to know details about everything. So I function as his New York *Times,* his CNN, his *National Inquirer,* catching him up on what the rest of the world's been doing while he concentrated on making the homes of the world beautiful."

NOT ONE BANDIDO IN 20,000 MILES

A Remembrance by James Johnston

I've kept a detailed record, and, according to my journals, the two of us have put 20,000 miles on the odometer in the last five years crisscrossing Mexico, a country we both love to distraction. Colorful and always surprising, scenically lovely, made lovelier still by the charm of its people, Mexico is an elixir to Beau—a revitalizing tonic, his fountain of youth. And I must admit, the opportunity to sip from Mexico's *copa de oro* also makes me a very happy man.

James Johnston

Prior to 1992, we traveled exclusively by air to our various Mexican destinations. But Beau decided the only way to see Mexico—the only way to shop Mexico—is on the ground, traversing the region coast to coast, border to border, in either van or truck, depending on how much he planned to buy and haul back to Texas.

His favorite season to be combing the length and breadth of the country is wintertime, specifically the days surrounding Christmas, when Mexico City is decorated at its most spectacular, all dressed up for company. And, just down the road, the Hotel El Tapitio in Guadalajara has the best bells and whistles to ring in the New Year.

. . . he always does what he says he will do . . .

We take out-of-the-way roads through jungles and primitive villages; we drive the skinniest, most winding mountain trails; we take in the sights; we appreciate the exotic—and sometimes very raw and difficult—nature of Mexico. Reports of bandits on the back roads are exaggerated. Fortunately for us, our trips have never been spoiled by desperados. More germane to the Beau experience in Mexico is that, no matter where we are, we keep our eyes peeled to find spots where something wonderful is for sale.

197

James and Beau dine with street vendors.

Often other friends come along for the ride. Beau will announce, "Today we'll look for the village of the wonderful rugs," and even though we do not know where he is taking us, we all expect the adventure will lead to bounty. Once the hidden enclave is discovered, we pile out of the van and follow our leader as he negotiates with local artists and artisans. His Spanish is as impeccable as his discernment of what is trash and what is treasure, so the shoppers on board usually come away with the unusual at an unusually good price.

Beau's connection with Mexico is very intricate, more complex than simply a nice place to shop. He has installed the country comfortably in his soul. He has taken the people to heart. I think, if bandits ever do pop out at us from the palm groves, they will wind up not only as his friends, but quite possibly he will give them all jobs.

A Car Window On The World

We have traveled along the eastern coast of Mexico from Tampico down to Vera Cruz, where the road cuts through thick banana groves, where the giant fruited stalks are wound in net wrappings preparatory to cutting and being hauled off to market.

Taking the high mountain road on the way to Jalapa, we've seen calla lillies growing wild, even pushing up through the rocks that line the roadside. We make summer trips to Monterrey and Durango and cross the green tabletop mountains that overlook Mazatlan. We like to drive a little south of Puerto Vallarta to a restaurant appropriately named Chico's Paradise, where we lunch beneath a palapa and listen to the relaxing sound of a running stream.

Loving the western coast as we do, we will drive one hundred miles south of Acapulco to Huatulco, hire a boat and cruise around until it's time to make the drive over the mountains to Oaxaca. It's a pristine and exquisitely preserved colonial Spanish town where the streets are so clean a casually dropped gum wrapper doesn't stand a chance. It'll be whisked away in mid-air by one of Oaxaca's city-proud citizens. The example is not an exaggeration, but an eye-witness account!

Beyond Oaxaca, we visit the village of Arrazola, famous for its artisans who create the whimsical woodcarvings, painted with vividly colored spots, outlandish zigzags, and markings never seen in nature. Still, these artifacts have captured the imagination of collectors worldwide and are produced by a small colony of people who seem to have the same skewed, but delightful, sense of humor.

Then on to Puebla and the Camino Real Hotel that, in the seventeenth century, functioned as a convent. Going on from saintly and into unsightly, we are in agreement that if we never again see Manzanillo it would be too soon. Even though Las Hades (made famous as the setting for the film *10*) sits whalebone-white out there on the peninsula, Manzanillo itself makes Nuevo Laredo look like the Champs Élysées.

To clear our vision of the eyesore, we travel north of Acapulco to Estapa Zihuatanejo— a lovely village set in a cove. Down close to the water waits the charming hotel, Villa del Sol—a unique edifice, gorgeously landscaped all around. We cannot change into bathing suits fast enough, hurrying to the beach where a line of shaggy-topped palapas invites us to lounge the day away, toes in the sand, cool drink in hand. Beau loves the place so much, he christened his home in Austin with the name of this paradisiacal setting.

Just before sunset, a bunch of kids, who are busily digging for chiquiliquis (little crawfish-type creatures), wave us over to join in the fun. Beau and J. T. prove to be quite good at the sport, but when I tried digging down into the sand to capture some of the delicacies, a crab caught hold of my finger. I yelled loud enough to wake Montezuma's ghost, but was successful in quickly flinging the thing away. Laughing, Beau said, "James got rid of it so fast and threw it so far, I thought he had a grenade!"

In Search Of Taco Stands And Picasso

Just as New Yorkers eschew the C-word when chatting about the Big Apple, denizens do not say "City" when speaking of the capital of Mexico. That can be quite confusing to visitors to the region. Imagine standing on a terrace that overlooks Acapulco Bay and being asked if you have ever been to Mexico. Naturally, you respond, "But I'm in Mexico at this present moment." It is then explained that "Mexico" is Mexico City to everyone, apparently, except you. After a quarter of a century of visits to the fair land, I still say "Mexico City" when I want to talk about Mexico City, and I want to talk about Mexico City. About Beau and Mexico City . . .

We enjoy making trips there, and as many times as we've visited, rarely have we varied our agenda. If we are on our own, and the trip has nothing to do with business, it is our custom to walk the same beaten path. The best explanation for this is that when Beau finds something he likes, something deemed flawless, perfect, he wisely sticks with it.

We arrive on Friday. Without hotel reservations. Once we reach the Zona Rosa section of Mexico City, he then decides which of two hotels he regards equal in perfection we will check into. Either the Segovia, which is a small and charming boutique hotel, or The Royal, which is larger, more luxurious. No preplanning, the choice is made on the spot, spur of the moment. Then it's off to dinner. In fifteen years of Friday night dinners with Beau in Mexico City, we've never eaten anywhere other than the Parri Pollo. I think he would feel compelled to wrestle anyone to the ground who tried to lure him away from Parri Pollo on Friday night. He's crazy about the exceptionally prepared chicken—charcoal grilled with seasonings that lift the pollo, and ourselves, to rapture.

Saturday morning we tour the upscale flea market located in the Zona Rosa. Every time we go, there is always something different, something that captures his interest. Beau has hauled a lot of stuff out of that flea market. We breakfast at Sanborn's—the drugstore atmosphere indicative of his allegiance to food and food service presented without any fussiness. (If the truth be told, The Brownstone is the only four-star restaurant Beau frequents. Not just because he owns it and the food is great, but because he's allowed to wear Bermuda shorts.)

200

Bazar Sabado—discovering the artist Juan Carlos Breceda with great friend and client Angela "Teensie" Blum

After stuffing our sacks with knockoff Lalique, brass, statues, wall hangings, and gewgaws at the flea market, it's off to Bazar Sabado, located in the San Angel district. The area of fabulous old homes, walled and dripping with bougainvillea, sits between two plazas, at the center of which artists display their paintings. A Spanish colonial church constructed in the seventeenth century adjoins one of the plazas, giving a backdrop of regal and venerable distinction to the art show.

It was here in this setting that Beau discovered the man he named "The Mexican Picasso." As many of Beau's clients will attest, Juan Carlos Breceda does paint in a Picassoesque style, mixing vibrant color into humorous and primitive images. Many of Breceda's ladies are posed with chickens sitting atop their heads. One gets the impression, when studying the eyes of Breceda's painted ladies, that they are staring out at a world imagined to be just as strange as the canvas world they live in. Also, the various citizens inhabiting Breceda's canvas world have a roundness that suggests they have not been underfed. Perhaps, after wearing the chickens on their heads awhile, they boil them up in aromatic oils and eat them. Beau loves the work of Breceda, and has functioned as his number one patron for many years.

We roam around for hours looking over the new crop of work by Mexican artists. When Beau begins inching in the direction of the Taco Lady, I know it's lunchtime. For as long as I can remember, she is always found seated behind her small charcoal brazier cooking chicken and potatoes, beef and beans, and wrapping up one or a combination of all inside handmade tortillas. Legendary for his cast-iron stomach, my friend Beau loves to dine with street vendors. The Taco Lady reciprocates the warm greeting extended by her best customer, and after we are perfectly satiated, we bid farewell to Bazar Sabado and return to the hotel to look over the loot.

The colors of Mexico: Beau and J. T., Mexican shirts, Mexican art

Sunday dawns. These days it is common for driver and good friend Cecilio to arrive from Acapulco, driving a big, roomy van. By the end of Sunday, Cecilio's van will be packed to the roof with acquisitions.

We wander over to Parque Sullivan, a square near the Zona Rosa reserved on this day for artists. It's very elegant and very beautiful, with winding sidewalks banked by flowering trees and shrubbery that provide a singular showcase for the aspiring artists. As pretty as the Rive Gauche must have appeared when the great (and undiscovered) impressionists of the nineteenth century stacked their canvases along river's edge, Parque Sullivan draws a sophisticated crowd. Men wearing suits and ladies in lovely dresses promenade through the cool morning air, giving respect to the gathered artists, and oftentimes, discovering genius among the canvases.

Beau buys many artworks on a Parque Sullivan Sunday, and Cecilio loads them up for transport either back to Acapulco or to the border, where Beau's wonderful purchases pass under the eagle-eyed inspection of border guards, who by no stretch of the imagination are art connoisseurs, and then are hauled up to Houston and the Brownstone Gallery.

202

By lunchtime our eyes drift from things aesthetically appetizing over to the bright orange tents that flap over an outdoor food market. Set contiguous to the art show, the stalls and crates and countertops in the marketplace display an abundant array of fruits and vegetables, peanuts, meats, fish, and exotic comestibles indigenous to the region. There are also food vendors. Because we have a favorite among the food vendors, the course of our Sunday never varies. We take a casual stroll over to the nice young couple whom the Epicurean gods have blessed with the enviable ability to whip up a very delicious shrimp ceviche.

Then, with reluctance, it's home to Texas. Home to add details to my journal, home to dream about our next trip south. Home to write Beau another in a long line of notes about my fondness for that young couple's ceviche. There will be words of thanks and admiration included at the end, but they are unnecessary. Beau knows how much I love him.

Ixtapa Zihuatanejo—Hotel Villa del Sol with the shaggy-topped palapas

Splendid Visions
VILLA DEL SOL

SOUL TO SOL

An ideal embraced by ancient sages and seers, who certainly saw more of unobstructed vistas than we moderns see today, acknowledged that to gaze upon an immense expanse of space is sublime and could best be appreciated from a hilltop. It wasn't by chance that Buddhist temples, for example, were constructed in the high hills; the builders understood that consciousness expands when there is room to breathe, where there is a fine view of the wide, open spaces.

And by the vision splendid
Is on his way attended…

—William Wordsworth

When Beau built his home 450 feet up from Lake Travis, he chose the site for its expansive, expressive range of beauty. In the positioning of Villa del Sol, Beau nailed sublimity right on the head. From the terrace there are views. From every point in the villa—no matter in which direction one looks—something of enchantment meets the glance and holds it. With beauty being all around, the viewer is mesmerized, and sighing is a natural reaction. At Beau's house, the aesthetic experience is very much like the sun passing the baton to night. When beauty sinks in, the soul is engaged.

The rough sketch for Villa del Sol was first drafted on a cocktail napkin. Dining out one evening with his friend Juan de Dios (J. T.) Trevino, Beau speculated on the proportions and appointments of a personal residence that would define his conception of perfection. Inspired, but without draftsman's tools to render inspiration into form, Beau improvised. Giving substance to imagination, he drew with a ballpoint pen upon a flimsy small square of paper that had, on the reverse side, an advertisement for some murky English ale. Perhaps not the most auspicious beginning for an edifice that would one day be compared to the elegant villas that grace the hillsides of Tuscany, but the idea was born. Villa del Sol took up residence in his mind.

The plan needed executing, however, and that is how Wayne Beaty came into the picture. For more than twenty-five years, Wayne had worked as building contractor on private residence projects for Beau's clientele. When the time came to begin conferring on the dream home that would be constructed for Beau himself, Wayne knew the collaboration had every chance of being their most challenging to date.

*Every detail of the design of Villa del Sol is meant to promote
comfort, a sense of beauty, romance, an appreciation of classicism,
and a relaxed response to the environment.*

The rough sketch for Villa del Sol was first drafted on a cocktail napkin.
Giving substance to imagination, Beau drew with a ballpoint pen upon a flimsy square
of paper that had, on the reverse side, an advertisement for some murky English ale.

Villa del Sol left me awestruck. Beau built a world-class structure— a home that you would expect to find overlooking the Mediterranean. It has a presence that complements its builder.

—Tom Theriot

The living room at the Villa del Sol houses Beau's collections of a lifetime.

Anticipating Beau's structural magnum opus to unfold in stages, with the work in progress progressing without constraint of unalterable architectural plans (only the most rudimentary plans allowed, and only allowed because they were needed to obtain a county permit), Wayne got ready to go with the flow.

Beau's vision would be delivered in chapters—chapters open to revisions, new revelations, to "Eureka" shouted now and again. Many changes would be made on the original thought, for the course of the visionary does not run smoothly. The best can always be a little better. Inspiration rarely finds itself added to a ledger sheet. But always factored into Wayne's world is the luminous magnitude of his friend's imagination. After working with Beau for many years, the contractor not only figures in the ever-whirling wheels of the creative process, but is credited with inventing a name for it: The Beau Factor.

The Beau Factor

Q: *Is The Beau Factor something that came up during construction of Villa del Sol, or had you encountered the phenomenon on other jobs as well?*

Wayne: It's always been there, just in varying degrees. Whenever we work together, I take into account that it's probable Beau will come up with several new wonderful ideas, necessitating a change of plans, and I will need to be adaptable.

Q: *For Beau, nothing is set in stone.*

Wayne: It's best not to do a lot of planning on a Beau project, as it can and will be played with variations on the theme. Fluidity is basic to the nature of an artist. I bet Michelangelo did not know the end result of every painting. I suspect what eventually made it to the Sistine Chapel ceiling surprised even him. An artist envisions and re-envisions his way through, and that's the way with Beau. Inspiration comes from some place other than the paintbrush or an architectural plan. The work is spirit-led.

Q: *How does Beau's approach to designing differ from that of other interior decorators you've worked with?*

Wayne: The majority of designers train themselves to do one thing. Their work is readily identifiable based on a singular style technique, which is often influenced by design magazines or decorator books. The shortcoming is a lack of flexibility. A lot of decorators miss the fact that homeowners are not all created alike. Beau designs to fit the client's personality. His resources are vast, his knowledge profound, his ability to visualize instantaneous and on the mark, and he doesn't need magazine pictures to guide the process. Room design takes place inside his head, with the vision honed to the pleasure of the homeowner. It's a talent and sensibility not universally held by other designers.

Villa del Sol, perched 300 feet above
Lake Travis in the Texas hill country,
takes you to another time, another place.

212

I think spending so many happy times on that hill in Acapulco inspired him to build the villa on the mountain in Austin.

—Ulysses La Grange

You could be on the Dalmatian coast.

—Beau Theriot

Q: *Was the creative process during development of Villa del Sol similar to other projects?*

Wayne: The two main elements definitive of Beau's creativity were always at work: his confidence and his fearlessness. The way he mixes textures and elements in structure, colors and furniture, patterns and periods—if anybody else tried it, they'd make a mess. To describe Beau's approach with Villa del Sol or any project, I would say that every phase is a new world, every room is a new world. An undiscovered world that he means to chart and settle.

Q: *You did not build Villa del Sol based only on the cocktail napkin sketch. There were formal plans.*

Wayne: Beau hired an architect who produced five sheets of architectural drawings. The drawings served two purposes. The first was to determine how big the house would be, if it would fit the lot. The second purpose was to have something to present to the county so we could get a permit.

Q: *As the creative process moved along, the five sheets were thrown to the wind?*

Wayne: It's been my experience that the first time most clients can really see a home is after the home is built. Drawings are one-dimensional, and most people—because they cannot truly envision the finished structure—stick religiously to the plans. Beau can see the end result when a project is still just on paper. He can see it before it gets to paper. Many times I've seen him do three-dimensional drawings on the job site. He'll grab a piece of wood or a brown paper bag, start sketching, then take the drawing to a field worker and say "This is what I'd like to see happen here." The guy, whether stonemason, electrician, or woodworker, looks and says: "Yeah, I see exactly what you want." For Villa del Sol, we worked more by Beau's sandwich bag sketches than architectural plans.

Q: *After a good working relationship between the two of you for many years for many clients, was there any butting of heads during construction of his very own personal dream home?*

Wayne: We fussed about steel. Beau thought I was overdoing it, putting in too much steel support. I asked him to trust me—and on construction of the veranda, he did. Because of the huge pieces of steel I used for the underpinnings and foundation, we were able to give him almost everything he asked for. For example, original plans for the veranda did not call for marble floors, marble walls, or stone columns. When Beau decided he wanted to switch to marble floors, marble walls, and stone columns, we were prepared. We had the steel in place to support the extra weight.

Only once did I have to say, "Can't do it," and that was when he wanted to change the wood columns in the dining room to stone columns. Unfortunately, we didn't have the support in that part of the house.

Because of the huge pieces of steel I used for the underpinnings and foundation, we were able to give him almost everything he asked for.

—Wayne Beatty

214

Constructing a villa the size of Villa del Sol on the edge of a steep hill was a challenging project. Some said it couldn't be done, but Beau knew better. The villa is living proof!

Q: *You were with him when he made the trip to The Boneyard?*

Wayne: Most amazing thing I've ever witnessed. The Boneyard is called that because it's a dumping ground for broken stone, for oddly shaped stone, for stone that was incorrectly cut. We went out there with a couple of trucks, and Beau began selecting and purchasing pieces bit by broken bit. Then we filled the trucks with every kind of stone imaginable—all mismatched, all varying in color. We hauled the pieces back to the site, unloaded, spread the pieces of stone on the ground, and Beau set to work constructing a Villa del Sol jigsaw puzzle.

By the time the house was finished, every piece of stone he had purchased had been used. Flooring, walls, window trim, fireplace, countertops—Beau found a place for every piece he'd hauled away from The Boneyard.

Q: *The building of Villa del Sol was a crowning achievement for Beau, personally and professionally.*

Wayne: I think Villa del Sol is reflective of the maturity of his abilities. It's one thing to have a gift, but it's another thing to utilize that gift through the years until it finally matures into excellence. Excellence is where he is.

A Walkabout

A stroll with Beau around the inside and outside of Villa del Sol turns the head of even the most nonchalant member of the group. To stand awestruck and pop-eyed is not uncommon. As a matter of fact, there are some veterans of the stroll, friends who have walked through the house with Beau many times, who will spot something wonderful that was overlooked on previous visits, and their eyes pop all over again. The pleasures of his taste are discovered in the pleasure of his company.

Inspired by the sunburst gate behind which Merle Oberon's Acapulco showplace, Sol y Mar, was secluded, the massive wrought-iron gate at the entrance to Villa del Sol replicates the design but does not the bar the way. Loving the sun and the lifestyle that attends all places where the sun is adored, Beau lets the sun shine in, and seclusion is not on the agenda. The showplace Villa del Sol is owned by an open-gate kind of fellow. Delighting in the tease, especially when the tease is spiked with truth, Beau says, "Hang a gate in front of a property and suddenly it looks like a million-dollar home."

He builded better than he knew:
The conscious stone to beauty grew.

—Ralph Waldo Emerson

Landscaping on both sides of the slate-blocked driveway showcases native Texas plants and brilliant flowering clusters of color; intermittent among the garden rows are statues and fountains, with the sound of running water a recurring theme at Beau's house. An arbor reminiscent of where classical Romans sat when they wanted to sit in a classical Roman summerhouse is located off the kitchen, and can be viewed from the driveway down a pathway planted with bougainvillea, oleander, weeping willow, and philodendrons.

One of Beau's classic cars graces the driveway at the villa. Twenty-five Texas-based stoneworkers were employed in construction of the house, which boasts stonework crafted in both abstract forms and in carvings recognizable in nature, such as the sunbursts around the windows.

Down the driveway and a slope that curves in the direction of the lake appears a drive-through garage that could generously accommodate more than fourteen vehicles. Beau calls it the world's biggest carport.

218

Villa del Sol was used in the filming of Robert Rodriguez' movie Spy Kids starring Antonio Banderas.

*At the age of twenty-seven, Beau was rummaging around his favorite shopping haunt
Snooper's Paradise, located near hometown Port Arthur, when he came upon two
paintings of curious, yet appealing, subject matter. This is one of the paintings, signed by
artist Millet and dated 1881; it seems to be a scene of happy dissipation in which the
revelers are enjoying the Belgian countryside. In the foreground of the pastoral setting,
a man appears wearing the bonnet of his lady friend. The two ladies in the scene—one of
whom is hatless—are smoking opium from dainty pipes, and the other male character
has such a deliciously goofy look on his face that it must be assumed he's already had
his pipe and smoked it too. The other painting is a scene of rowdy merriment inside a
Belgian tavern. Both masterworks measure 8 feet × 8 feet and now hang with prominence
in Villa del Sol, where they continue to be a source of great delight for the collector.*

The view from the gate back across
Comanche Trail Road is of the hill opposite,
which slopes down into a vineyard where vines
hang heavy with purple and raspberry-colored
grenache and shiraz grapes that will eventually
be harvested and bottled under The Oasis label.
"The limestone soil here is similar to the soil
in Australia, where these grape varieties thrive,"
Beau says.

West of the vineyard stretches a 350-acre
panorama of pristine hills and forestland.
Undeveloped, with a plan in place to remain
undeveloped, the acreage has been given to the
birds. When Beau gave the area to the state of
Texas for the establishment of a perpetual bird
sanctuary, he kept the view in view. Though his
entrepreneurial spirit vied with his sense of
beauty in the allocation, Beauty won.

Stonework, crafted in both abstract form
and in carvings recognizable in nature, such as
the sunbursts etched around windows, gives
character to the facade of Villa del Sol. A carving
of the six flags of Texas crowns the structure in
tribute to the native soil from which so many
interesting individuals have sprung. It was created
by a favored group of artisans in Guadalajara,
from whom Beau frequently commissions work.
Twenty-five Texas-based stoneworkers were
employed on the home front to bring their
industry and artistry to the construction of the
house. Comprising 10,000 square feet, Villa del
Sol took a year and four months to be completed.

Bypassing the front door, Beau decides
instead to first lead his guests on a stroll around
the exterior, taking them down the driveway.

They then go down a slope curving in the direction
of the lake. He enters an area that is, arguably, the
first floor of Villa del Sol and appears at first glance
to be a drive-through garage that could generously
accommodate more than fourteen vehicles.
"World's biggest carport," Beau calls it.

Kidding aside, the section belongs heart and
soul to the overall home and, for several reasons,
should not be viewed as a detachment. Art has
not been neglected. Stone carvers have been
busy detailing and adorning walls and portals.
Beautifully crafted arches frame French garden
statues, lions gurgle water in the fountains,
trompe d'oeil paintings add happy caprice to
convention, plants healthy with a surfeit of
chlorophyll cascade down the sides of massive
bronze planters. From the Frio River have come
the polished cypress beams overhead. On the
lake side of the concourse there are several
apartments and a game room. Directly across the
drive are the wine cellar, a bathroom constructed
specifically for the needs of the physically
impaired, and one of three utility rooms.

Often converted into a tunnel of fun, the
first floor pavilion is the best place to set up buffet
tables and is more than adequate for arranging
attractive seating areas for three hundred to dine.
With lots of room left over for bustling waiters,
mingling guests, strolling mariachis, and cordial
young ladies carrying trays of flutes bubbling with
champagne, the space is a natural for throwing
a party. Cooled by breezes blowing front to back
as well as drawing breezes off the lake, and with
the extra attraction of Beau's collection of classic
automobiles, this is, indeed, some carport!

The stained glass windows salvaged from an old Texas church
color a thoughtful carrera marble cupid on the stairs.

The opposite end leads to an area designated for a future swimming pool and attendant cabanas. Beau has sited the pool area at the very edge of the hill providing a beautiful overlook of the lake, in a style consistent with his preference when plotting spatial design for his homes in Acapulco. Enchanted by the optical illusion that segues state-of-the-art construction with natural lake view, the designer plans to put in a negative-edge pool. "Besides being beautiful, edgeless pools have a mystical, ethereal quality, as if you are floating above the world, without a safety net," says Beau.

A three-story circular tower Beau dubbed "The Wine House" flanks the recreational area. The first floor wine-tasting room may also be utilized for intimate dinner parties; the second and third floors have been designed to function as boutique suites for guests. Appointed with handmade Italian tile inside, the outside stone construction ascends to a turret, in complement to the romantic Old World look Beau wanted to achieve for this freestanding structure. With its copper roof, stained glass windows, and antique doors, The Wine House is charmingly detailed.

Beau points out a circuitous driveway that leads down to the lake, but cautions that it is steep and precarious and requires "a strong golf cart" to manage the hill going down and for chugging the way back up. He recommends walking the trail only to the hardy of limb and determination. As an aside, he encourages those who have packed hiking boots to make the trek for the spectacular views.

A meander around the west side of the house leads through the Roman belvedere, down the garden path, and returns again to the front of the house. Escorted through the soaring glass and iron antique double doors, guests enter a vestibule.

The view elicits an immediate sensory reaction. The best spontaneous response overheard upon entering the foyer was, "If Heaven looks like Beau's house, I'm going to change my ways immediately!"

Just as a swan's neck has a graceful subtlety, the interior of Villa del Sol does not overwhelm, does not beat one about the head with an insistence that it be regarded the grandest of the grand. Instead, it creates a sensation of familiarity, a feeling that it's okay to touch stuff, that shoes may be kicked off even if the shoes will land on the floor of a palace.

"They were inviting me to probe a new thought, and I imagined that I had to identify an old memory," wrote Marcel Proust. The French novelist's words are profoundly applicable as regards the synergy that has been achieved at Villa del Sol. New thoughts and old memories live together comfortably here—both the past and the present (and one or two items futuristic) coexist in harmony. Wit and wisdom go hand in hand.

Beau's style is generally described as informal classicism, but the classicism leans toward the suggestion that design has been rendered by a barefoot boy with cheek. Mythological creatures frescoed across the ceiling overhead look down upon a one-of-a-kind solid bronze chandelier that weighs in at a walloping twelve hundred pounds. Forward of the entry hall, the staircase railing ascends in a gentle curve, its composition simple and unadorned save for subtle intervals of ironwork. Beau adds the comment that the use of bird's eye maple on the stairs "keeps everything from becoming too serious."

Stained glass windows salvaged from an old Texas church manage to have the same muted primary colors used by the artist responsible for the scene of ribaldry depicted in one of Beau's favorite paintings. Occupying its own wall in the living room, the exuberant painting was purchased in the collector's youth for a song. Its value now approaches grand opera.

To the left, between the vestibule and the living room, a spacious black marble bar room is located off the promenade, and beyond that, a cozy niche for reading or doing desk work. But this is no ordinary study. Even bill paying must be fun at such a desk, which is attended by a pair of throne chairs from a French castle. The Louis XVI desk, opulent with gold gilding and substantial but gracefully curved and carved legs, was purchased when the savvy designer was on a shopping trip in Paris at the youthful age of thirty-one. The desk is one of those treasures Beau held back from the showroom floor at the Brownstone Gallery, hoping that one day it would grace the halls of his own private residence.

A two-step descent leads to the living room's polished wood floor, which was constructed from an old pecan tree found at the Theriot family haven, Whippoorwill Farm. Floor-to-ceiling bookcases made of pinewood line the far wall, centered by a stonework fireplace designed by Beau. To the right of the fireplace, hidden behind a little pop-off board at the edge of the bookcase, is the key to opening the secret door. Eyes filled with fun, Beau asks, "What's a home without a secret panel hiding a secret room?" A peek inside reveals a dark staircase. Beau insists the room at the top is a very nice apartment with all the modern conveniences, and he swears it's completely ghost-free.

High glass windows interspersed with sliding doors grace the easternmost walls of Villa del Sol, allowing views of the lake from the whole of the interior. From the thresholds of the living room, bar, and dining room, guests walk beyond the looking glass, stepping out onto the exquisite sweep of the terrace, where colonnade and fountain, fireplace and water-spouting gargoyles share artistic space with museum-quality statues. The railing, configured of waist-high glass panels rimmed in iron, runs the seventy-three-foot length of the terrace and assures clear views whether the viewer is standing or seated in one of the four conversational vignettes. A peaceful, gorgeous place to pass the time, to watch the clouds float by, to gaze down at the lake and see the sailboats gliding by.

Beau purchased the Louis XVI desk on a shopping trip in Paris at the youthful age of thirty-one, hoping that one day it would grace the halls of his own private residence.

Beau feels that a round dining table is the most conducive to good conversation.

Sipping cocktails on the terrace . . .

The terrace is so beautiful it could be a movie set. When Austin's famed writer/director Robert Rodriguez had a script that called for elegance on a grand scale, he brought his crew to Villa del Sol to shoot scenes for *Spy Kids*. Recounting the celluloid experience, Beau says, "It took the crew a day to set up. There were wires everywhere, hundreds of people roaming around the house; the scene was a perfect combination of excitement and chaos.

"When the cameras finally started rolling, we watched Antonio Banderas, his costars, and a gang of extras do the wedding scene. We heard Melanie Griffith off-camera requesting I find an ashtray for her cigarette, saw J. T. enlisted to be a movie actor for a day. (J. T. was taller than Banderas). And when the movie came out, we all piled in the car, zipped down to the shopping mall theatre, bought tickets, and in a packed audience made up of people all under age twelve, we saw J. T. on the screen for maybe a second. But the terrace was prominently featured in the film."

Laughing at the memory, Beau glances up to the left where the stacked decks of The Oasis zigzag down the side of the hill. With hundreds of umbrellas unfurled and the sound of music wafting down, the gigantic restaurant/recreational facility shares its festive mood with those gathered on the terrace. It's a roosting place for waterbirds who have flown up from the lake, for tourists and regulars who keep coming back for more after the weekend sunsets, dancing to music under the stars. "Six months a year, three nights a week, we can sit right here on the terrace and enjoy the music coming from The Oasis. And over there and under the trees," Beau says, directing all eyes down the right side of the lakefront, "is the only officially designated nude beach in Texas."

Reentering the house, someone asks Beau the origin of the mammoth stone figure, Bacchanalian in subject matter and presumably very old.

He says, "I found it at Marche aux Puces de Saint-Quen, the famous Paris flea market and a favorite place to shop. To haul it to this spot took the grunts and groans of thirteen very strong men."

Once again positioned in the entry hall, we can now explore the gallery wing of the main floor. A small painting by Marc Chagall, illuminated by art light, has an inscription, "Pour Elsa," written in the artist's own hand; Beau identifies Elsa as Chagall's wife. Under the stairway, a lacquered grand piano faces the main dining salon. No ordinary instrument this, but a ten-foot ebony concert grand from Estonia, which was formerly a part of the Russian Empire. "I love great pieces from *todo el mundo*—all over the world," says Beau.

227

On display in the dining room at Villa del Sol are two original paintings by Spanish artist Edouard Cortez depicting beautiful scenes of Paris. Beau bought the paintings in 1978 at an auction in New Orleans without knowing anything about the eminently collectible artist. Beau turned the winning bid because he recognized the beauty of the works, a talent that has been repeated all through his collecting history. One of the works is extremely rare because of the appearance of the Eiffel Tower in the background; although Cortez is appreciated for his renderings of the tower, its appearance is strangely limited in his works.

The family room at the villa is better known as Señor's room.

Proceeding into the dining room, guests realize that the host prefers to dine by circumference. Beau likes dinner guests gathered Arthurian-style around a round table, rather than squared off or seated perpendicular. It's more convivial, he says, to see eye-to-eye and to create a current of conversation that breezes around unobstructed by angles. As one wit noted in passing, "It's tough to spot a love triangle at a round table."

Just off the dining salon, the entrance to a professionally equipped catering kitchen looks across at the wall opposite to a neon art piece that must be the most futuristic work displayed in the house. Behind the kitchen's swinging door is every chef's dream—a state-of-the-art playground for cooking. A high ceiling looks down on a silver streak of stainless steel. There are two sub-zero glass-door refrigerators; an oven fit for a professional kitchen; and three separate double-sink areas for coffee preparation, for cooking by the stove, and a deep-dish double-sink for washing hundreds and hundreds of dishes. The brick floor is overlaid with thick rubber that is aerated with holes, giving a spring to the step of kitchen workers.

In the walk-in china cabinet are three 250-piece sets of china, chafing dishes, baskets, decorated pots, gadgets and gewgaws, doilies, patterned everyday napkins, fine linen, two dozen sets of napkin rings (both formal and whimsical), and everything else imaginable to throw a humdinger of a party.

The most futuristic piece of art work displayed in the villa is by the well-known Texas artist Ozuna.

Exiting through a door at the opposite end of the catering kitchen, the tour group enters a home kitchen that is barrier free, looking out upon a room that holds comfort in highest regard. "This is Señor's room," Beau says. Asleep currently, almost hidden in the soft down of the couch, Señor seems in perfect accord with his master's proclamation. This is one contented Chihuahua.

Bookcases behind Señor's couch were made in Great Britain of old English pine and procured from a London craftsman. Columns from the eighteenth-century Georgian period are of interest to a guest, who expresses admiration for the mixing of different woods, different stonework, and textures of fabric throughout the home.

Continuing on through the exercise room and around to the back stairs, a whoop of delight from the strollers is heard when they come upon the leopard skin carpet leading up to Beau's bedroom. This being the back entrance, and being apparently freely accessed from the hallway below, a question is posed regarding privacy. "What do you do when you want to go to bed, and the party is still raging on below?" Beau pushes a button. Hidden from detection, and descending from a slim and elongated slot above, a partition slowly, mechanically slides down to the floor and privacy is achieved.

Sometimes we see a cloud that's dragonish;
    A vapour sometime like a bear or lion,
A tower'd citadel, a pendant rock,
    A forked mountain, or blue promontory
With trees upon't . . .

—William Shakespeare

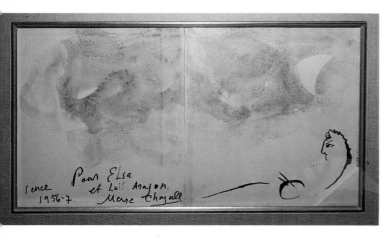

Eyes go to the burnished red and snow white color combination of real fox fur that stretches across the width of the bed in the master suite. One must control the urge to throw oneself on the fur and roll around in the soft pelts. Even though Beau's schedule does not permit extended lounging around in a bedroom filled with earthly delights, when he does get to relax, all the comforts of home await him in this room. Designed to stimulate a feeling of ease, comfort nestles up against the aesthetic. Both are compulsory.

Beau loves chandeliers. On the third floor of Villa del Sol are three bedrooms: the master and two guest suites. Ceiling elevation varies in the three rooms, ranging from fourteen to twenty feet and allowing lighting fixtures to be dramatically displayed.

In the guest suite that overlooks the terrace and the lake, the chandelier is rock crystal and iron and was forged in Spain.

Off the dressing room in the lake-view suite, the bathroom features a floor-to-ceiling tiled shower spacious enough to wash a four-man polo team and one horse. Those of shy and modest leanings need not apply for permission to shower here. The oval picture window stretches from the ankle to the top of the head, keeping no secrets from the boaters below.

The selection of paintings for the lake-view suite is a mixture of European street scenes and mythic Grecian themes in muted pastels. Across the hall, paintings rich in primary colors grace the walls of the second guest suite and are focused on human form and face. Original paintings by Breceda, Cortez, and Gerald McCann fill the wall space, creating the feeling of being in an artist's atelier. Beyond the canopied bed, a charming sitting room overlooks the vineyard and the rolling hills of the bird sanctuary.

The hallway leading from the bedrooms ends at the grand staircase. A pause seems in order to allow the eyes to review the splendors of Beau's vision. "Come on, my friends," says Beau, with more beautiful notions up his sleeve, "tour's over. Now let's go out on the terrace and drink champagne in the moonlight."

Contentment with his place in time and space often inspires a song. Singing as he descends the stair, "The stars at night are big and bright, deep in the heart of Texas," Beau shows us that it's true. The big bright Texas stars do twinkle above, reflecting his home in all facets of its beauty. Yet, the real treasures of Villa del Sol cannot be seen in art or artifact; they are the cherished and enduring friendships that are kept deep in the heart of Beau.

Beau's friendship with Señor is a cherished and enduring one. For Señor, attitude is everything!

Man's Best Friend And Coworker

Beau's friendship with Señor is one of those enduring friendships. "Señor! Let's go!" is a familiar call—one that the debonair Chihuahua responds to with the imperturbable air of an old campaigner. Whatever the mission, wherever they might be headed, whomever they may be going to visit, when Beau says it's time to hit the road, Señor trots gamely forward.

At first observation the two pals—a statuesque man, a very small dog—might seem an unlikely match. In his bare feet, Beau measures six feet four inches. Standing next to those feet, even at his most erect, even with head held high and legs stretched to a military stance, Señor is no bigger than a popcorn box. But attitude is everything. Beau might tower over his canine friend as mountain to molehill, but the feisty, faithful lad is not intimidated. Some people are tall, some are not. Señor is very philosophical about the matter.

To understand the bond between the two, one must understand that Beau and Señor share the same work ethic as well as mutual admiration. Committed to being on the go from sunup to sundown, they will grab a quick bite mid-day—Beau likes soup, Señor a soup bone—then, in a flash, they're off and running again.

Making it known to Beau early in their relationship that he could never be content to lead a dog's life, Señor is no malingerer. He doesn't try to duck out of a job, never barks in sick, never hides behind the Louis Quatorze couch to avoid responding to his master's voice. Instead, he's just as eager as Beau to get the day going at full throttle. Pacing around at the front door to make sure he's not left behind when Beau grabs the keys, Señor is the one who leads the way out to the car. Leaping up and in, he scrambles to his regular perch inside Beau's SUV. Standing with rigid purpose atop the car's console, Señor is as much a permanent fixture as the hood ornament.

Nothing, not a rolled Aubusson infringing on a portion of his space, not a leaning flower vase nor a chair leg, could move Señor off his sacred spot. As packed as Beau's SUV invariably is with fabric samples and garden statues and rugs and things rococo destined for homes of clients, there is always room for Señor. It's a sacrosanct and first priority both in Houston as well as Austin. The loyal Chihuahua doesn't miss a beat or an installation. "If I were Señor," says friend-client-dog fancier Mary Laminack, "I'd see that my name was added to the payroll."

Revelations and Reflections
ONCE AND FUTURE DREAMS

SHINING PROSPECTS

The development of the five hundred acres known as Comanche Canyon Ranch can be described as a dream-in-progress. When Beau shared his dream with business consultant Shirley Shaw, neither anticipated that the dream might be called upon to do battle with nightmare. Many years would pass, during which the good thought tried to hold its own against bad mojo. With stumbling blocks, red tape, insect infestation, avian angst, and recalcitrance from many sectors thwarting progress, development of Beau's acreage in the far west Austin hills has been slow-go.

I like to walk about amidst the beautiful things that adorn the world...

—George Santayana

A close friend of Beau's for twenty-two years and business consultant for fourteen of those years, Shirley went to the front of the line when it was time to board the roller-coaster ride of the Comanche Canyon Ranch project. Endowed with a sharp intellect and the sort of no-holds-barred imagination that complements Beau's thinking process, Shirley works under two official titles at the Austin office: Director of Advertising and Public Relations for The Oasis, and Vice-President of Development for Comanche Canyon Ranch.

In an unofficial capacity, Shirley also lends her professional singing voice to informal occasions, being the one Beau will ask to perform when friends are gathered and the night calls for music. A member of seniority within Beau's intimate group of traveling companions, she has ventured with him across the world, for shopping and for the pleasure of discovering what's over the next hill. Established between them is a comfortable friendship of tenure, accented with laughter, gilded with shared experience.

But, when it comes down to serious business, their focus of interest has long been riveted on Comanche Canyon Ranch. Impediments to its development began fourteen years ago when an Austin bank turned down Beau's request for a loan. As collateral he had offered the pristine expanses of the property he owned free and clear. The bank, being unmoved by possible endangerment to struggling entrepreneurs, gave its sympathies instead to the birds and the bugs.

The Villa del Sol is located on the five hundred acres Beau owns on Lake Travis. The area will be developed into a nature preserve, vineyards, and homes of architectural similarity with their own views of the lake.

A study was under way at the time to determine if a specific bird species should be listed as endangered. Given sanctuary by the United States Fish and Wildlife Service in 1987, the black-capped vireo was granted permanent refuge on Beau's property. Then, in 1988 the uncertainty of the status of a bug species called the karst invertebrates crawled into the picture. The decision of the federal government was that the bugs should also be protected. By 1990, another bird species, the golden cheek warbler, warbled its way to notice, winning a third place on the endangered list.

The future was uncertain, not only with regard to the use of the land for collateral, but also the eventual development of the property.

The battle with the government stretched into a ten-year war. For a decade, there were debates to be waged, setbacks to be endured, meetings to attend, contentions to be contended with, bureaucrats to cajole and persuade.

Over the years of negotiations—years that required diplomacy and a great deal of savvy—Shirley and Beau persevered. In 2000, the federal government granted Comanche Canyon Ranch a 10-A permit, which meant development could proceed, but only with the guarantee that the birds and bugs would be protected. Victory, though not sweet, seemed in reach. With nays somewhat defeated, the ayes of Texas and the feds were finally upon them.

I remember the day of Esther Smith's birthday party. We had planned to drive from Austin to Dallas to attend the formal affair, but late in the afternoon Beau called the office and asked me to make arrangements for a private plane because there was no time to drive, and he was determined not to miss celebrating his friend's birthday. The only place I could find a plane was at the little Georgetown (Texas) airport, which was the only small airport in the vicinity that had runway lights for landing when we returned later that night.

Dressed, I sped over to Beau's house to pick him up for the thirty-five-mile drive to Georgetown. Beau came out wearing his brand new tuxedo and looking very handsome, but I noticed he kept hitching up his pants. I asked, "What's the matter?" He took his coat off, explaining that he had not tried on the pants (Beau's clothes shopping method is to just hold stuff up—he never tries anything on).

He showed me that he had rolled the pants up at the waist—he'd rolled the waistline over at least three times—then he had tied the cummerbund tightly around the triple rolls.

When we finally arrived at Esther's, Beau looked fine and I was happy that no one could see how he'd rigged the pants. However, as is the way of my fun-loving friend, halfway through the party, he took the tux jacket off and paraded the fact that he'd neglected to schedule an appointment with the tailor. Beau loves a laugh, even if it's on him. Never did get those pants fixed.

—Shirley Shaw

Teamwork

Q: *As a team, you and Beau fight dragons well together.*

Shirley: Our methods are different, but we are equally passionate in our will to win. From Beau's standpoint, it's bothersome to have someone tell you what you can, or what you cannot, do with your own land. The demanding procedures required by agencies of the government make no sense to Beau. The process is slow and frustrating, and Beau is not a man who likes slow. Also, he's not one who is fond of things unreasonable, and unreasonable is sometimes the nature of the bureaucratic beast.

Best friends and colleagues Beau and Shirley

Q: *At one point, you were threatened with losing the whole of the five hundred acres.*

Shirley: Yes, initially the U.S. Fish and Wildlife Service determined that the entire acreage would have to be designated a wildlife preserve and we would not be allowed to develop any of the land. Once that news got out, The Nature Conservancy came to us and offered a little over a thousand dollars an acre—secured with one hundred dollars earnest money. We did a lot of hair-pulling, gnashing of teeth, and moaning during that period.

Q: *How was it eventually resolved?*

Shirley: It took time for the bugs and birds to be officially deemed endangered, then more time for us to win the 10-A permit, fourteen years of time. I visited with anyone in government who would give me an opportunity to plead our case—from United States federal agencies to Travis County agencies to the officials from the city of Austin. Finally, at the turn of the twenty-first century, under the auspices of a newly formed entity called the Balcones Canyonland Conservation Plan, we were told we could use certain parts of the land for development, as long as we kept the rest of the acreage sacrosanct for wildlife. Resolution: three-hundred-fifty acres out of the five hundred will remain, into perpetuity, a preserve.

Q: *On the plus side, people who eventually reside on Beau's mountain will have the extraordinary experience of living in the midst of a natural paradise.*

Shirley: Yes, once the gorgeous structures are built, there will not be a bad view from any window in any house. But even paradise comes with restrictions. Because it's been determined that the preserve should not draw the wrong kind of birds, people who buy the lots will see a clause in their deeds that specifies what kind of bird feeders and what kind of birdseed they are allowed to have. I have no idea what penalty will be exacted if the bird police discover a rogue feeder.

Q: *In 1988, the property was located out in the wild, wild west. Is it now designated as being within the Austin city limits?*

Shirley: No, but the official boundary of the fully annexed city limits is just a mile away, so not only has the area ceased to be the wild west, but we're not even suburban anymore. Being semiurban, we see a flock of inspectors and permit people, city officials, and county regulators in the area daily. Ten years ago, we might see one person once a month.

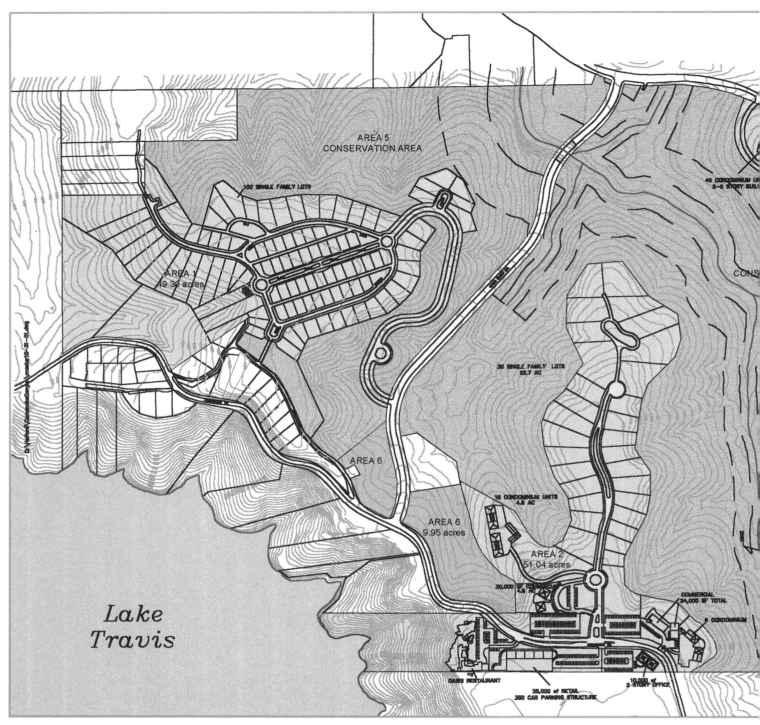

Lake Travis

AREA 5
CONSERVATION AREA

100 SINGLE FAMILY LOTS

AREA 1
49.30 acres

AREA 6

AREA 6
9.95 acres

30 SINGLE FAMILY LOTS
22.7 AC

18 CONDOMINIUM UNITS
4.6 AC

AREA 2
51.04 acres

30,000 SF COMMERCIAL
4.6 AC

COMMERCIAL
24,000 SF TOTAL

6 CONDOMINIUM

OASIS RESTAURANT

28,000 sf RETAIL
350 CAR PARKING STRUCTURE

10,000 sf
2 STORY OFFICE

COMANCHE CANYON RANCH 468.88 Total Acres		
AREA	LAND USE	ACREAGE
1	Residential: 100 Single Family Home Sites	49.30 ac.
2	Residential: 30 Single Family Lots 24 Condo Units Commercial/Office: 5 Bldgs- 64,000 Sq Ft Total Restaurant: 2600 seats Retail: 10,000 Sq Ft Parking Structure: 350 spaces	51.04 ac.
3	Residential: 2 Single Family Lots 40 Condo Units 24 Town Home Units	11.58 ac.
4	Residential: 21 Single Family Lots	20.72 ac.
5	Conservation Area	326.29 ac.
6	Vineyard	9.95 ac.

Plan of land use for the development of Comanche Canyon Ranch. The green portions, approximately three-fourths of the ranch, are set aside by Beau as a nature preserve.

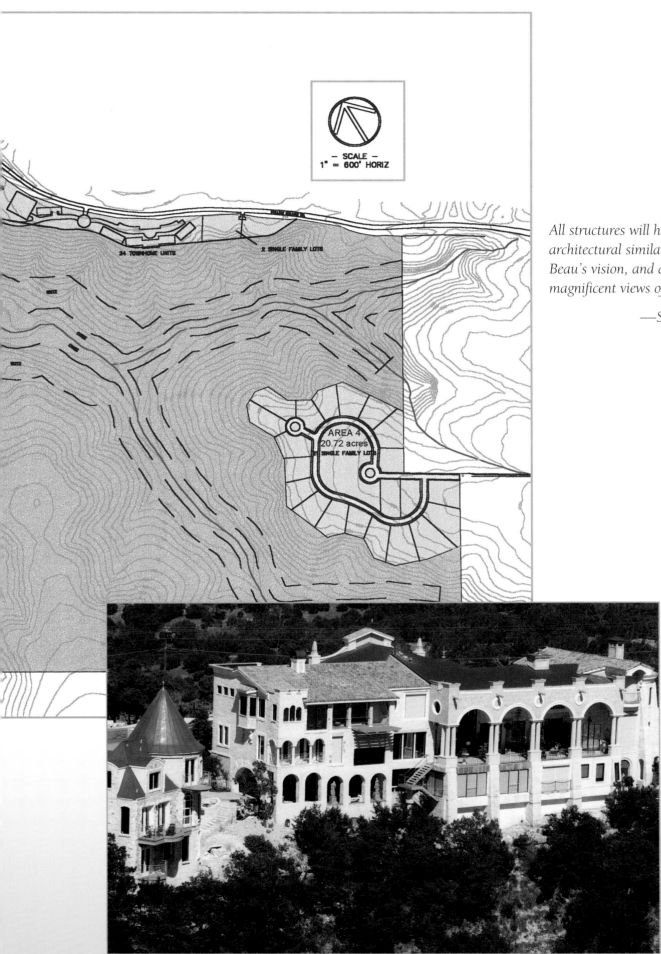

— SCALE —
1" = 600' HORIZ

24 TOWNHOME UNITS

2 SINGLE FAMILY LOTS

AREA 4
20.72 acres
21 SINGLE FAMILY LOTS

All structures will have an architectural similarity based on Beau's vision, and all will have magnificent views of the lake.

—Shirley Shaw

Q: *Have the areas for residential and commercial development been sectioned off and approved by the powers that be?*

Shirley: Our proposed development boundaries are drawn, and now we wait to see if our estimates are accepted by the city of Austin. We anticipate having to do some bargaining on some of the residential boundaries. But once that's done, then the areas for housing projects can be surveyed and our residential sites will be finally, firmly, set in stone. At that time, Beau plans to deed over the conservation acreage to the Balcones Canyonland Preserve.

Q: *Any plans for building a big convention hotel with an eighteen-hole golf course in the commercial area—in the area near The Oasis?*

Shirley: No, Beau's not comfortable with a project of that scale—a hotel complex is too sprawling and too impersonal. Throughout his career, Beau has always drawn the greatest joy from personalizing a creative project. The best way to understand his vision for the property is something I've heard Beau express many times. He says, "As I stand at the front door of Villa del Sol and look over the mountain, the structures that will be built take form in my mind—I can hardly wait to see the dreams become reality." Every aspect of architectural design, aesthetic accoutrements, symmetry, and sensibility of the Comanche Canyon Ranch development will rise out of Beau's sense of beauty.

Q: *Will you build in phases?*

Shirley: As currently planned, we'll first break ground on the hilltop off Oasis Bluff. With upscale lake view lots on the perimeter, interior lots will flow together as a beautiful garden home community. All structures will have an architectural similarity based on Beau's vision, and all will have magnificent views of the lake. There will be fifty traditional homes, with fifteen most unusual, most dramatic three-story dwellings, narrow and tall, with walled fronts and glass back walls that look out on the lake. The structures will be gated and sophisticated. The first phase is called Villa Montaña, and it's Beau's baby.

Q: *Will architectural design stay consistent with the shining prototype of his own home, Villa del Sol?*

Shirley: Yes, there will be a consistency in mood and theme, line and textures—aesthetically harmonious. For someone born in East Texas, who was not exposed to classic design and décor as a child, Beau is as comfortable with the surroundings of Villa del Sol as a French lord. While many may be overwhelmed by the treasures collected in his home, Beau knows the name and designation of each piece, the value then and now, knows origins and history. I think he was born with the knowledge, born with good taste.

Q: *Is the plan for commercial area building projects to be taking place simultaneously with residence developments?*

Shirley: The Treasury, completed in the summer of 2002 and located across the street from The Oasis, is Beau's interior design gallery. It has three stories comprising 15,000 square feet, with two floors of wonderful home furnishings, art, and artifacts; and the third floor is designated for corporate offices and Beau's private art collection. The parking garage adjacent to The Oasis will be more than just a parking garage. Wrapped with 25,000 square feet of specialty retail stores designed to resemble a European village, this project is currently under construction. On the same side of the street as The Treasury, two buildings will be erected in the style of classic European wineries. One of the buildings will be a charming, terraced cafe that shares space— if my own personal dream comes true—with a tabletop store, selling table settings exclusively imported from Italy.

Beau and Shirley on a buying trip to Italy

Q: *Why limit your merchandise to Italy alone?*

Shirley: Because of the buying trips. I would like my job description to clearly state that it's absolutely imperative that I make buying trips to Italy twice a year!

Q: *Any other development planned in the vicinity of The Oasis?*

Shirley: Yes, down the hill from the winery buildings there will be eighteen townhomes that overlook the vineyard. Our aim is to create a charming village—for shopping, dining, and residing in a most unique setting.

Q: *You plan to develop in phases.*

Shirley: Taking the entire project into consideration, we forecast a four-phase development. Villa Montaña, first phase; second phase, the vineyard townhomes and thirty single family lots—a gated community near the winery buildings. Third phase will be in the vicinity of Bullick Hollow and will comprise two five-story lofts that have a total of forty units, twenty-four townhomes that will have beautiful views of the canyon, and two estate lots. For the fourth phase, located at the east end of the property near Highway 620, we plan to build twenty-one large single family homes. All development is estimated to be completed over a ten-year period.

Of course, that forecast is much too slow for Beau. He would prefer all phases to begin at once, and, if the wish could truly be father to the action, he would like the entire mountain developed overnight. After waiting so long to get started, Beau's ready to see those castles rise in the sky from the vantage point of his front porch.

What's really fun is to go with him into a dark and cluttered warehouse—a place where 95 percent of the stuff is junk, nothing you would ever want to take home. Way back in the poorly illuminated recesses, way back in a corner, there will be a single exquisite piece. Beau will walk straight to it.

—Shirley Shaw

One of Beau's favorite things is sharing his life and his homes
with friends. The purple and raspberry-colored grapes that
grow on the slope across from the villa serve as the cover for an
invitation to celebrate at Villa del Sol.

Villa del Sol

*Please come and spend an enchanting Indian Summer afternoon
of camaraderie with my family and friends
in the Texas Hill Country.*

*Honoring my wonderful sisters, Dianne and Brenda
and their November birthdays, as well as
all the great ladies in my life.*

*I wish to share with all of those that I love the blessings
and the great freedom we have as Americans.*

Come be a part of the celebration!

No gifts please, you are welcome to bring a friend and a bottle of wine.

Beau
Villa del Sol
6638 Comanche Trail at Oasis Bluff
(Next to THE OASIS)

Sunday Nov 11, 2001
4:00pm to 8:00pm
Casual Lake Chic

RSVP Ask for D.J. or Terrine

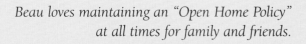

*Beau loves maintaining an "Open Home Policy"
at all times for family and friends.*

VIEWS FROM THE TERRACE

Reflections by Beau Theriot

Beau holding up the Leaning Tower of Pisa

There are very few things that fail to delight me, although I admit to not liking people who paddle their boats with rakes; people who swallow camels and choke on gnats; frilly food; an untended garden; horror movies; wasting anything, from time to money to friends; jobs half done; bureaucracy; brains wearing blinders; group decisions; society balls and dressing formally; computers; liver; hard pillows; hard heads; late arrivers; and planning for the future.

A lot of things delight me, delight me so much that I wager even senility could not erase a continued enthusiastic appreciation. I will always remember joy—small joys, middle-sized joys, and the big kicks too. Like everyone, I keep in mind—cherish in mind—the favorite places, favorite events, favorite things, favorite sights and sounds and tastes, favorite people (and that's quite a list!) that have made life wonderful.

Reflecting over the past years, recollecting the high points and the low points, visions came sweeping in, bringing chuckles, bringing tears, bringing sighs, smiles, and a few frowns. I began creating a list of memories.

May I suggest you also indulge—take the time to remember the times of your life. Use the blank back page of my book to write. One day we'll all get together and compare notes!

Take the time to remember the times of your life.

A Few Of My Favorite Things

A gorgeous, ageless room; a gorgeous, ageless woman; a gorgeous, ageless man.

The Taj Mahal—the world's most exquisite building. A most magnificent structure of perfect proportion erected in the perfect setting. Who can forget the brilliance of sculpted white marble duplicated in the reflection pool?

Pan Am Flight 101 stopped at such marvelous places as the Taj Mahal.

Pam Am Flight 101. It flies no longer, but once you could go around the world in 2 1/2 days, stopping at nine destinations—Los Angeles to Hong Kong, Singapore, Bangkok, New Delhi, Karachi, Athens, Rome, London to New York. What a trip! I made it twice, but not in 2 1/2 days. The best part about Flight 101 was that I could hop off, look around, shop around, stay a few days, then catch the plane when it made the next swing by. Of all the wonderful things lost to the world, I wish for the return of Flight 101.

The Petronas Twin Towers in Kuala Lumpur, designed by architect Cesar Pelli. A wonder seen while visiting the Malay Peninsula, and unforgettable.

The desert air. I can still feel it, still feel the tiny grains of sand sting my face as we rode horses out to see the pyramids in Egypt. As mystical and mystifying as being lost in the bazaar in Marrakesh. I dream of returning to both places.

*B*uenos Aires, even though the city reminds me of a once-pretty woman who has had too many face-lifts that went wrong, and now wears cheap jewelry because she had to pawn the good stuff, but there's still an attraction in the old broad.

*P*laces in the world where they do not speak English—the ultimate in exotic travel.

*F*rench antiques—eighteenth century armoires with the patina of old warm woods, whether softly carved or grandiose with heads of mythic creatures. My majestic bureauplat, found in Paris, now installed at Villa del Sol. I am a sucker every time for the style and the period.

*A*ll antique carved pieces of furniture that have withstood the scars of time, wonderfully patinated and softly glowing.

*L*ooking for treasures in the Paris Flea Market and the Parque Sullivan in Mexico City.

*C*reating a stunning room for an appreciative client—or even for an unappreciative client.

*C*lients who listen to me.

Beau and J. T. in France

*I*mari and Rose Medallion porcelains.

*B*ig pull-up ottomans.

*D*esigning a romantic mood for the boudoir.

The purple and raspberry-colored grapes that grow on the slope across from the Villa del Sol.

Mornings in the gallery, looking forward to Carmen's famous mango smoothie. (Looking forward to any opportunity to taste Carmen's cooking!)

Soup. All kinds, all concoctions, anytime, anywhere. Soup for nourishment of the heart, mind, body, and soul.

Guacamole (Oh, why be limited! Tex-Mex all the way!) and freshly caught redfish cooked on a grill set in the sand at the primitive beach in Acapulco.

Mom's pot roast and country vegetables, Ann's banana pudding, sister Dianne's chicken cooked in wine sauce, Myrt's tiny pecan pies, J. T.'s fried eggs sunny side up, Carmen's great crêpes, Modesta's Key lime pie.

Beau with some of his favorite friends: J. T., Señor, and Milagro

My friend and serious business partner Señor looking into my eyes at quiet times, watching my every move when we're out working . . .

And our very good friends, J. T. and Milagro.

Maintaining an "Open Home Policy" for family and friends.

Spending every Christmas with the family at Mom's saltbox house in the Texas Piney Woods. Walking in those woods in East Texas with my family, enjoying the flora and fauna.

Cool, clear autumn mornings.

A colorful, triumphant sunset to mark the end of another incredible day.

Cymbidium orchids, wild roses, lilies, begonias, Australian tree ferns, bougainvillea.

Huge beautiful trees spreading their branches over rocky hill country creeks.

Mexican artist Breceda is one of Beau's favorite discoveries.

Finding the mirror used in the movie *Hush, Hush Sweet Charlotte* in an antique store in New Orleans, bringing it home, and hanging it in the ladies' powder room at Villa del Sol.

Architecture of Antoni Gaude and Frank Lloyd Wright—peerless, creative imaginations.

Mexican artist Breceda's chicken-headed women and Picasso's three-eyed, three-breasted women.

Original creations—whether of stone, clay, glass, bronze, wood, or paper—I appreciate what the artist can imagine and create.

The substantial: big carvings of rock and wood, heavy wrought-iron gates, hefty hinges, carved balustrades, important window trimmings, soaring columns. There is a sense of anchoring that comes with these things.

The skill of Mexican stoneworkers.

Black and white sketches—simple, direct, uncomplicated, a true representation of the artist's degree of talent.

Classic cars: classic T-Birds, Rivieras, Super Sports, and Caddies from the '60s.

Driving a classic convertible through the great U.S.A. Driving everywhere: The world is a highway meant to be explored.

Natural smiles, sparkling eyes, great posture.

The play, the songs, the characters, the message of *Evita*. I am awed by the genius of Andrew Lloyd Webber.

A Fish Called Wanda, in my opinion, the funniest movie ever made. Second favorite funniest movie: *To Wong Foo, Thanks for Everything, Julie Newmar.*

The casual flair of my Hawaiian shirts.

Poetry—good or not so good—I love it all.

Wicked humor. Make me laugh, and I'll follow you around forever!

Sharing—cards and letters written with personal thoughts, expressions of love, humor, remembrances, promises that we will meet again soon.

It's no secret, especially now that you've read the book, that I like to live 100 percent in the present. Nothing more boring than wondering and worrying about what will happen two years from now. Much more fun to be surprised! And of equal excitement—to do a couple of surprising things myself.

Beau ✳✳✳